What Is...
Stark Law?

DONALD H. ROMANO, EDITOR
JONATHAN E. ANDERMAN
MATTHEW R. FISHER

D1474905

AMERICAN BAR ASSOCIATION
Health Law Section

Printed in the United States of America.

18 17 16 15 14   5 4 3 2 1

Cataloging-in-Publication data is on file with the Library of Congress.

ISBN: 978-1-62722-441-3

Discounts are available for books ordered in bulk. Special consideration is given to state bars, CLE programs, and other bar-related organizations. Inquire at Book Publishing, ABA Publishing, American Bar Association, 321 N. Clark Street, Chicago, Illinois 60654-7598.

www.ShopABA.org

Contents

CHAPTER 4
Penalties and Compromise   57

About the Editor

Donald H. Romano is Of Counsel to Foley & Lardner LLP, in the firm's Washington D.C. office. He counsels clients on regulatory compliance matters, particularly those pertaining to the Anti-Kickback Statute, the physician self-referral statute (Stark Law), HIPAA, and the Medicare enrollment regulations. He also advises hospitals and other providers and suppliers on Medicare reimbursement issues. Prior to joining Foley & Lardner LLP, Mr. Romano was a partner in another D.C. based law firm, and prior to that he had over 25 years of experience in the Department of Health and Services, including as a senior attorney in the Office of General Counsel, and as a Division Director in the Centers for Medicare & Medicaid Services. In that latter position, he was responsible for, among other things, Stark policy, Provider Reimbursement Review Board procedures, and the Anti-Markup Rule.

Mr. Romano is a frequent speaker and author on health law topics. He is a past chair of the American Bar Association Health Law Section's Interest Group on Fraud and Compliance, and a past vice-chair of the American Health Lawyers Association's Regulations, Accreditation and Payment Group. He earned his J.D. from the University of Baltimore in 1984 and his B.A. from Towson University. He is admitted to the bars of the District of Columbia, Maryland and Massachusetts.

About the Authors

Matthew R. Fisher is an associate with Mirick O'Connell in Worcester, MA. Mr. Fisher is the chair of the firm's Health Law Group and a member of the firm's Business Group. He focuses his practice on health law and all areas of corporate transactions.

Mr. Fisher's health law practice includes advising clients with regulatory, fraud, abuse, and compliance issues. With regard to regulatory matters, he advises clients to ensure that contracts, agreements and other business arrangements meet both federal and state statutory and regulatory requirements. Mr. Fisher's regulatory advice focuses on complying with requirements of the Stark Law, Anti-Kickback Statute, fraud and abuse regulations, licensing requirements and HIPAA. He also advises clients on compliance policies to develop appropriate monitoring and oversight of operations. In addition, he represents clients in all stages of business transactions, including formation, contract review and preparation, and mergers and acquisitions. Mr. Fisher assists clients of all sizes from small closely held companies to large multinational companies.

Mr. Fisher is active in the ABA Health Law Section. He holds various leadership positions and helped develop and implement the Health Law Section's social media efforts. Mr. Fisher was named a Massachusetts "Super Lawyer" by Boston magazine and Law & Politics in 2013, and a Massachusetts "Rising Star" in 2011 and 2012.

Mr. Fisher earned his J.D., *magna cum laude*, from Suffolk University Law School and his B.A. in Political Science from Haverford College.

Jonathan E. Anderman is an associate in Holland & Knight's Boston office and a member of the firm's Healthcare & Life Sciences Team, White Collar Defense and Investigations Team, and Corporate Mergers and Acquisitions Group. He advises clients on healthcare regulatory matters, on fraud, abuse, and compliance matters, and on corporate transactional matters in various sectors of the healthcare industry, including pharmaceutical and medical device manufacturers, pharmacies (retail, specialty, long-term care and mail order), pharmacy benefits managers, insurers, venture capital and private equity investors, and e-health and technology companies. Mr. Anderman represents clients in internal investigations and in matters before state and federal regulatory and law enforcement authorities, such as the Department of Justice, United States Attorney offices, State Attorney General offices, and the Office of the Inspector General of the Department of Health and Human Services. He also assists in a variety of corporate and contractual transactions for healthcare and life sciences companies, including mergers and acquisitions, financing, product development and supply, licensing, technology transfer, joint ventures, and various other service and supply chain transactions.

In addition to his practice, Mr. Anderman is active in the healthcare industry and in the community. He was named a Rising Star by Massachusetts *Super Lawyers* in 2013 and holds leadership positions with several organizations, including the American Bar Association, Health Law Section. He also writes and speaks frequently on health law and general legal topics. Mr. Anderman is a 2012 graduate of LeadBoston, an executive leadership program focused on civic engagement and social responsibility. He has an active *pro bono* practice, including extensive work on post-Katrina legal issues in New Orleans.

Mr. Anderman earned his J.D., *cum laude*, from Boston University School of Law and his B.A. in Biology, Genetics, and Bioethics from the Pennsylvania State University.

Introduction

The Physician Self-Referral Law, commonly known as the Stark Law (42 U.S.C. § 1395nn), prohibits a physician from referring Medicare patients for certain services defined as designated health services (DHS), to an entity with which the physician or an immediate family member of the physician has a direct or indirect "financial relationship." The law also prohibits an "entity," such as a hospital or other provider or supplier, from billing for DHS furnished as a result of a prohibited referral.

The Stark Law is a strict liability law, which means that no intent to violate the statute is necessary for claims for DHS to be denied or a violation to be found. Despite Stark being a strict liability statute, there are enhanced penalties for knowing violations. Specific statutory and regulatory exceptions protect certain relationships from the law's general prohibition. If a referral relationship does not meet each and every requirement of an exception, liability attaches to a prohibited referral. As such, whenever an arrangement involves a financial relationship with a physician who refers designated health services that are payable by Medicare,[1] the proposed arrangement must be evaluated for compliance with the Stark Law based on the specific facts and circumstances.

---

1. The statute was amended in 1993 to make Stark applicable to Medicaid, but no regulations have been issued implementing the amendment. Accordingly, most experienced Stark practitioners believe that there are no penalties associated with referrals for Medicaid services until such regulations are issued.

Before undertaking a detailed analysis, it is important to determine if the proposed arrangement even implicates the Stark Law. Health care attorneys typically perform a four-question assessment when presented with a potential Stark issue:

(1) Are designated health services referred by a physician to an "entity"?
(2) Does the physician or a member of the physician's immediate family have any financial relationship with the entity furnishing the designated health services?
(3) Will the Medicare program be billed for the services?
(4) Will the proposed arrangement meet an exception to the Stark Law?

If the answer is "no" to any of the first three questions, the Stark Law is not implicated. If the answer to the first three questions is "yes" and the answer to the fourth question is "no," the arrangement, as proposed, would not comply with the Stark Law, and should either be abandoned or be altered to satisfy an exception. Conversely, if the answer to the fourth question is "yes," the proposed arrangement complies with the requirements of the Stark Law and can be implemented. It is important to note that an arrangement need only satisfy one applicable exception, and the parties do not need to declare or identify that exception before implementing the arrangement. However, parties are advised to carefully structure an arrangement with one or more of the exceptions in mind before putting an arrangement into practice.

This book presents a general overview and discussion of the Stark Law. Chapter 1 provides an overview of the statute itself. Chapter 2 highlights the regulations, specifically a number of the most commonly used regulatory exceptions, and explains the terms of the exceptions as well as providing limited discussion of their application. Chapter 3 explains the source of interpretations of the Stark Law, including key cases and advisory opinions. Chapter 4 provides an overview of enforcement mechanisms and consequences for violations of Stark. Finally, the book includes a list of resources to further assist attorneys as they research and analyze Stark issues.

The Stark Law

1

In 1989, Congress enacted the Stark Law, named after then–California Congressman Fortney "Pete" Stark, to address the perceived problem of physician self-referrals, which Congress described as the practice of a physician referring Medicare clinical laboratory business to an entity with which the physician (or his or her immediate family member) has a financial relationship. Congress's concern, in its most basic form, was that a physician who self-refers might overuse items and services paid for by Medicare to further his or her own financial interest, leading to both increased costs to the federal health care system and adverse impacts on patient care.

The Centers for Medicare & Medicaid Services (CMS), an agency within the Department of Health and Human Services (HHS), is responsible for interpreting the Stark Law and issuing regulations and other guidance. Through its oversight of the law, CMS has published a series of proposed and final regulations, together with extensive commentary, that implement and attempt to explain Stark (the "Stark Regulations"). The Stark Regulations both implement the statutory exceptions and, pursuant to statutory authority, set forth additional exceptions. In conjunction with the statute, these proposed rules, final rules, preambles, commentary, and other guidance create the complex legal and regulatory scheme that constitutes the Stark Law.

A. Statutory Background

What is commonly referred to as the Stark Law is found in Section 1877 of the Social Security Act, 42 U.S.C. § 1395nn. As mentioned above, instead of consisting of a single legislative enactment, it is a series of statutory and regulatory enactments from the past twenty-plus years. It began with the original physician self-referral law, commonly known as Stark I, which was part of the Omnibus Budget Reconciliation Act (OBRA) of 1989.[1] The only designated health services under Stark I were clinical laboratory services. Congress significantly expanded the scope of DHS with Stark II, part of the OBRA of 1993,[2] which took effect in 1995. By mid-1995 CMS (then called the Health Care Financing Administration)[3] published regulations interpreting and implementing Stark I.[4] The regulations made clear that most of its commentary and guidance would apply equally to Stark I and Stark II because Stark II had been enacted between the time of the proposed (1992) and final rule (1995).[5] Since the time of the 1995 Stark I final rule, CMS has published numerous sets, or phases, of regulations interpreting and implementing Stark II.[6]

B. Basic Prohibition

The Stark Law prohibits (1) physicians from referring patients for designated health services to an entity with which the physician (or

---

1. Pub. L. No. 101-239, 103 Stat. 2106 (1989).
2. Pub. L. No. 103-66, 107 Stat. 312 (1993).
3. For simplicity, CMS and it's predecessor agency, the Health Care Finance Administration, will hereinafter be referred to collectively as "CMS."
4. 60 Fed. Reg. 41914 (Aug. 14, 1995).
5. *Id.* at 41,916.
6. For simplicity and consistency, references to the Stark Law shall mean all versions of the law because all of its iterations have been fully integrated.

his or her immediate family member) has a financial relationship, and (2) the entity performing the designated health services from billing Medicare for any such referred DHS, unless a statutory or regulatory exception applies. Specifically, it provides:

> (1) In general
>
> Except as provided in subsection (b) of this section, if a physician (or an immediate family member of such physician) has a financial relationship with an entity specified in paragraph (2), then
>> (A) the physician may not make a referral to the entity for the furnishing of designated health services for which payment otherwise may be made under this subchapter, and
>> (B) the entity may not present or cause to be presented a claim under this subchapter or bill to any individual, third-party payer, or other entity for designated health services furnished pursuant to a referral prohibited under subparagraph (A).[7]

In order to invoke the general prohibition on self-referral, an organization must first meet the definition of an entity furnishing designated health services. Next, a financial relationship between the physician and the entity must exist. If the first two circumstances exist, and there is a referral for designated health services that will be billed to Medicare, it must be determined if the arrangement can meet an exception. If the proposed arrangement meets an exception, it is not prohibited and the services may be billed to Medicare for payment. If an arrangement is determined to constitute a financial relationship between a referring physician and an entity furnishing designated health services, and the arrangement

---

7. 42 U.S.C. § 1395nn(a)(1). For ease of reference, the parenthetical "(or an immediate family member of such physician)" will be omitted. Future references to "physician" in connection with the Stark discussion should be read to include the omitted parenthetical. An "immediate family member" or a "member of the physician's immediate family" is defined to include: husband or wife; birth or adoptive parent, child, or sibling; stepparent, stepchild, stepbrother or stepsister; father-in-law, mother-in-law, son-in-law, daughter-in-law, brother-in-law or sister-in-law; grandparent or grandchild; and spouse of a grandparent or grandchild. 42 C.F.R. § 411.351 (2013).

does not meet an exception, the arrangement will result in a Stark violation if the designated health services are billed to Medicare pursuant to a referral by the referring physician.

C. Key Statutory Concepts

1) Entity Furnishing Designated Health Services

The initial inquiry under the Stark Law is whether the organization to which the physician is referring Medicare business is an entity furnishing designated health services. In order to be an entity furnishing DHS, two components must be satisfied. First, the organization must be an "entity furnishing," as specified in the Stark Regulations. Second, the health service in question must be considered DHS as specified under the Stark Law.

An entity furnishes if it performs[8] services that are billed as designated health services and/or bills Medicare for the DHS. In addition to the "entity furnishing" component, in order to fall under the ambit of Stark, the health services furnished must be DHS. The Stark Law defines DHS to include:

+ Clinical laboratory services;
+ Physical therapy services;
+ Occupational therapy services;
+ Radiology services, including magnetic resonance imaging, computerized axial tomography scans, and ultrasound services;
+ Radiation therapy services and supplies;
+ Durable medical equipment and supplies;
+ Parenteral and enteral nutrients, equipment, and supplies;
+ Prosthetics, orthotics, and prosthetic devices and supplies;
+ Home health services;
+ Outpatient prescription drugs;

---

8. The statute does not provide a special definition for "perform," and CMS has also declined to craft a special definition of "perform" to date. Instead, in the FY 2009 Hospital Inpatient Prospective Payment System Final Rule, CMS stated "[w]e decline to provide a specific definition of 'perform,' but rather intend that it should have its common meaning."

- ◆ Inpatient and outpatient hospital services; and
- ◆ Outpatient speech-language pathology services.[9]

The Common Procedural Terminology (CPT) and Healthcare Common Procedure Coding System (HCPCS) code sets help identify the services and items that qualify as DHS or that may qualify for certain exceptions. The published list of CPT and HCPCS codes is updated annually in the Federal Register and is also posted on CMS's website.[10] It is also necessary to review the Stark Law and/or the Stark Regulations for special definitions of particular services. For example, the Stark Law's definition of "radiology services, including magnetic resonance imaging, computerized axial tomography, and ultrasound services" is defined as "radiology and certain other imaging services" in the Stark Regulations.[11]

2) Financial Relationships

There are two types of financial relationships within the meaning of the Stark Law.[12] The first is an ownership or investment interest, which may be through equity, debt, or "other means."[13] The second is a compensation arrangement, which includes remuneration between the physician and the entity furnishing the designated health services.[14] Ownership/investment interests and compensation arrangements may be direct or indirect. A more complete discussion of what constitutes a direct or indirect financial relationship can be found in Chapter 2, Section B. Remuneration is broadly defined and includes any payment or other benefit in cash or in kind that is not specifically excluded from the definition.[15] As will be discussed in greater detail in Chapter 2, the Stark Regulations add a great deal of complexity to interpreting the meaning of financial relationships.

---

9. 42 U.S.C. § 1395nn(h)(6)(F). Note, however, that the Stark Regulations contain the same list of DHS, but order the specific services slightly differently. *See* 42 C.F.R. § 411.351.
10. 42 C.F.R. § 411.351 ("List of CPT/HCPCS Codes").
11. See the definitions section of the Stark Regulations, 42 C.F.R. § 411.351.
12. 42 U.S.C. § 1395nn(a)(2).
13. *Id.* at 1395nn(a)(2)(A). An ownership or investment interest includes, but is not limited to, stock, partnership share, and limited liability company memberships, as well as loans, bonds or other financial instruments that are secured with an entity's property or revenue or a portion of that property or revenue. 42 C.F.R. § 411.354(b)(1) (2013).
14. *Id.* at 1395nn(a)(2)(B); 42 C.F.R. § 411.354(c).
15. 42 C.F.R. § 411.351.

D. Exceptions

As previously stated, the Stark Law is a strict liability statute and any deviation from its terms is a violation. Accordingly, for a proposed arrangement that would otherwise run afoul of Stark's general prohibition, it is essential to meet all of the elements of an exception. There are a variety of general and specific exceptions that, depending on the nature of the arrangement, may apply in any given case, and these exceptions are both numerous and constantly evolving. The statute contains certain of the exceptions, and the Stark Regulations both modify and expand upon the statutory exceptions. Given the overlap and detail provided by the Stark Regulations, Chapter 2 explores the exceptions in more depth.

Below is a brief summary of the exceptions as contained in the statute.[16] The summary is categorized by those exceptions that apply to: (1) both ownership and compensation arrangements; (2) only ownership or investment interests; and (3) only compensation arrangements.

1) General Exceptions That Apply to Both Ownership and Compensation Arrangements

The statute contains several exceptions to the self-referral prohibition that apply to both ownership or investment arrangements and compensation arrangements. The exceptions that apply to either type of financial relationship include:

- **Physicians' Services**—exempts physicians' services provided by a physician in the same group practice as the referring physician.[17]
- **In-office Ancillary Services**—exempts services, with the exception of most durable medical equipment services, that are: (1) furnished by a referring physician or member of the same group practice (or individuals under the direct supervision of those physicians); (2) furnished in a building where

---

16. This summary is only of the statutory exceptions. Chapter 2 discusses the regulatory exceptions.
17. 42 U.S.C. § 1395nn(b)(1).

the referring physician or others in the group practice furnish other non-designated health services, or furnished by a group practice member in a building used by the group practice for the provision of clinical laboratory services or for the centralized provision of the group's DHS; and (3) billed by the physician performing or supervising the services, by the physician's group practice, or by an entity wholly owned by the physician or group practice.[18]

- **Prepaid Plans**—exempts services provided by certain managed care organizations to members of qualifying prepaid health plans.[19]
- **Electronic Prescribing**—the statute also exempts electronic prescribing according to the regulation issued under authority of another provision of the Medicare statute.[20]

2) Exceptions for Ownership and Investment Arrangements Only

Next, the statute provides certain exceptions specific to ownership and investment arrangements. These include:

- **Publicly Traded Securities**—exempts ownership of investment securities that are purchased on terms available to the general public and listed on certain recognized exchanges, and are in a corporation with average shareholder equity (in the previous three fiscal years) of $75,000,000.[21]
- **Publicly Traded Mutual Funds**—exempts ownership of shares in a regulated investment company (i.e., a mutual fund) if the company had average total assets (in the previous three fiscal years) of $75,000,000.[22]
- **Hospitals in Puerto Rico**—exempts ownership or investment interest where designated health services are provided by a hospital located in Puerto Rico.[23]

---

18. 42 U.S.C. § 1395nn(b)(2).
19. 42 U.S.C. § 1395nn(b)(3).
20. 42 U.S.C. § 1395nn(b)(5).
21. 42 U.S.C. § 1395nn(c)(1).
22. 42 U.S.C. § 1395nn(c)(2).
23. 42 U.S.C. § 1395nn(d)(1).

- **Rural Providers**—exempts ownership or investment interests where designated health services are furnished by an entity in a rural area if substantially all of the DHS furnished by that entity are in such rural area, and, if the entity is a physician-owned hospital, it meets the grandfathering requirements elsewhere in the Stark Law.[24]
- **Whole Hospital**—exempts ownership or investment interests where designated health services are furnished by a hospital if the referring physicians is authorized to perform services at the hospital, the ownership or investment is in the whole hospital itself (not merely a specialty subdivision or service line), and if the hospital is physician-owned it meets the grandfathering requirements elsewhere in the Stark Law.[25]

3) Exceptions for Other Compensation Arrangements

The statute also specifies certain exceptions for other types of compensation arrangements. These exceptions include:

- **Rental of Office Space**—exempts the rental of office space if: (1) the lease is set out in writing, signed by the parties, and specifies the premises to be covered; (2) the space is reasonable and necessary for the legitimate business purpose of the lease and is used exclusively by the lessee; (3) the term of the lease is at least one year; (4) the rental charges are set in advance, consistent with fair market value, and do not take in account the volume or value of referrals or other business generated between the parties; (5) the lease would be commercially reasonable even if no referrals were made between the parties; and (6) the lease meets other requirements imposed by the Secretary to protect against program and patient abuse.[26]
- **Rental of Equipment**—exempts the rental of equipment if: (1) the lease is set out in writing, signed by the parties,

---

24. 42 U.S.C. § 1395nn(d)(2).
25. 42 U.S.C. § 1395nn(d)(3).
26. 42 U.S.C. § 1395nn(e)(1)(A).

and specifies the equipment to be covered; (2) the equipment is reasonable and necessary for the legitimate business purpose of the lease and is used exclusively by the lessee; (3) the term of the lease is at least one year; (4) the rental charges are set in advance, consistent with fair market value, and do not take in account the volume or value of referrals or other business generated between the parties; (5) the lease would be commercially reasonable even if no referrals were made between the parties; and (6) the lease meets other requirements imposed by the Secretary to protect against program and patient abuse.[27]

- **Bona Fide Employment Relationships**—exempts any amount paid by an employer to a physician who has a bona fide employment relationship with the employer if: (1) the employment is for identifiable services; (2) the amount of remuneration is consistent with fair market value and is not determined in a manner that takes into account (directly or indirectly) the volume or value of any referrals by the referring physician; (3) the agreement is commercially reasonable in the absence of any referrals from the physician to the employer; and (4) the relationship meets other requirements imposed by the Secretary to protect against program and patient abuse.[28]

- **Personal Service Arrangements**—exempts remuneration to a physician for personal services provided that: (1) the arrangement is set out in writing, signed by the parties, and specifies the services covered; (2) the arrangement covers all of the services to be provided by the physician to the entity; (3) the aggregate services are reasonable and necessary for the legitimate business purpose of the arrangement; (4) the term of the arrangement is for at least one year; (5) the compensation paid over the term of the arrangement is set in advance, consistent with fair market value, and not determined in a manner that takes into account the volume or value of any referrals or other business generated

---

27. 42 U.S.C. § 1395nn(e)(1)(B).
28. 42 U.S.C. § 1395nn(e)(2).

between the parties (except for certain incentive plans); (6) the services do not involve the counseling or promotion or business arrangements or other activities that violate any law; and (7) the arrangement meets other requirements imposed by the Secretary to protect against program and patient abuse.[29]

♦ **Remuneration Unrelated to the Provision of DHS**—exempts remuneration provided by a hospital to a physician if such remuneration does not relate to the provision of designated health services.[30]

♦ **Physician Recruitment**—exempts remuneration provided by a hospital to a physician to induce the physician to relocate to the area of the hospital to serve on its medical staff, if the physician is not required to refer patients to the hospital, the amount of remuneration is not determined in a manner that takes into account (directly or indirectly) the volume or value of any referrals by the physician, and the arrangement meets other requirements imposed by the Secretary to protect against program and patient abuse.[31]

♦ **Isolated Transactions**—exempts certain isolated transactions (e.g., one-time sale of property or practice) if the amount of remuneration is consistent with fair market value and is not determined in a manner that takes into account (directly or indirectly) the volume or value of any referrals by the referring physician, the transaction is commercially reasonable in the absence of any referrals from the physician to the entity, and the transaction meets other requirements imposed by the Secretary to protect against program and patient abuse.[32]

♦ **Certain Group Practice Arrangements with Hospitals**— exempts an arrangement between a hospital and a group under which designated health services are provided by the group, but are billed by the hospital if: (1) with respect

29. 42 U.S.C. § 1395nn(e)(3).
30. 42 U.S.C. § 1395nn(e)(4).
31. 42 U.S.C. § 1395nn(e)(5).
32. 42 U.S.C. § 1395nn(e)(6).

to services furnished to an inpatient of the hospital, the arrangement is pursuant to the provision of inpatient hospital services under 42 U.S.C. § 1395x(b)(3); (2) the arrangement began before December 19, 1989, and has continued in effect without interruption since such date; (3) with respect to designated health services covered under the arrangement, substantially all of the DHS furnished to patients of the hospital are furnished by the group under the arrangement; (4) the arrangement is pursuant to an agreement set out in writing that specifies the services to be provided by the parties and the compensation for the services; (5) the compensation paid over the term of the agreement is consistent with fair market value and any compensation per unit of service is fixed in advance and is not determined in a manner that takes into account the volume or value of any referrals or other business generated between the parties; (6) the agreement would be commercially reasonable in the absence of referrals to the entity; and (7) the arrangement meets other requirements imposed by the Secretary to protect against program and patient abuse.[33]

- **Payments by a Physician**—exempts payments made by a physician to a laboratory in exchange for the provision of clinical laboratory services or to an entity as compensation for other items or services furnished at a price that is consistent with fair market value.[34]

The Secretary of HHS is also given broad authority to create additional exceptions for other financial interests that do not pose a risk of program or patient abuse.[35] This authority may be used to fashion exceptions not explicitly set forth in the text of the Stark statute. As will be seen, the Secretary has used this authority to create the full list of regulatory exceptions.

---

33. 42 U.S.C. § 1395nn(e)(7).
34. 42 U.S.C. § 1395nn(e)(8).
35. 42 U.S.C. § 1395nn(b)(4).

Although the Stark Regulations provide greater detail and requirements for complying with an exception to Stark, it is still important to understand the exceptions as set forth in the statute. Even though it is more advisable to follow the terms of the Stark Regulations, it may be possible to raise a defense to a claimed violation by relying upon differences found in the plain language of the statute. Arguably, to the extent that the plain language of the statute is in conflict with the Stark Regulations or CMS's interpretation, the plain language of the statute should control.

Stark Regulations 2

The statutory text of the Stark Law is only the beginning of the law's implementation, interpretation, and enforcement. The Stark Regulations are the lifeblood of the statute and play the largest role in informing the health care industry of its requirements. The regulations both expand upon and modify the language of the statute. Although it may sometimes be possible to comply with Stark without understanding the nature and scope of the Stark Regulations, it is much easier to comply with the law if one has as full an understanding of the Regulations as possible. Without awareness or knowledge of the Stark statute and regulations, it can be perilous to advise clients who propose to enter into arrangements where designated health services will be referred by physicians to entities with which they have a financial relationship.

The Stark Regulations are found at 42 C.F.R. §§ 411.350–411.389. The regulations define terms, describe various types of financial relationships, set forth the requirements of the exceptions, describe how to request an advisory opinion, and present other related matters. The discussion in this chapter focuses on Sections 411.351 to 411.357, which govern the types of permissible ownership, investment, and compensation arrangements between entities and/or physicians who do or may refer patients for designated health services.

A. Regulatory History

The Stark Regulations were not issued all at one time, nor have the regulations remained static following their initial promulgation. To the contrary, CMS has engaged in numerous rounds of rule making. In fact, the regulations continue to be amended and modified periodically. The regulations provide one of the few opportunities to obtain CMS's view of the Stark Law and how it applies to practical, real-world scenarios. The various rounds of rule making, and occasionally only proposed rule making, tease out how exceptions to the Stark Law are applied, offer guidance as to what should be done to ensure that relationships are structured appropriately, and sometimes provide insights into where the government sees new compliance problems developing.

1) Stark I Final Regulations

The first round of Stark Law regulations was promulgated in connection with the original 1989 Stark Law (Stark I), which applied to clinical laboratory services only. The proposed rule was published in 1992,[1] and the final rule was published on August 14, 1995,[2] technically after Stark II, the expanded Stark Law, was enacted. The initial regulations only applied to clinical laboratory services since they were promulgated pursuant to Stark I, but helped to serve as the basis for the regulations to come as the definition and scope of designated health services were expanded. Concepts adopted in later rounds of regulations were set forth in the first effort. As such, the Stark I final rule is instructive in interpreting still existing portions of the regulations.

---

1. 57 Fed. Reg. 8588 (Mar. 11, 1992).
2. 60 Fed. Reg. 41,914 (Aug. 14, 1995).

2) Stark II, Phase I Regulations

The first round of regulations under Stark II was issued on January 4, 2001 (known as Phase I Regulations).[3] The Phase I Regulations did not take effect, for the most part, until a year later, on January 4, 2002. The Phase I Regulations addressed the general broadening of Stark to cover ten additional designated health services as opposed to the limited application (clinical laboratory services only) of the first regulations from 1995. The Phase I Regulations addressed the general prohibition on self-referrals, and also began the discussion of the service-based exceptions that apply to both ownership or investment interests and compensation arrangements, e.g., the in-office ancillary services exception. However, the Phase I Regulations purposefully did not address all aspects of Stark because future rounds of rule making were already anticipated. Overall, the Phase I final rule with comment period took a more industry-friendly approach in several respects as compared to what was proposed in the 1998 proposed rule.[4]

3) Stark II, Phase II Regulations

The second round of regulations under Stark II was issued on March 26, 2004 (the Phase II Regulations).[5] The Phase II Regulations, which became effective on July 26, 2004, responded to numerous comments received in connection with the 1998 proposed rule by broadening or revising some exceptions and creating additional exceptions, i.e., exceptions not contained within the language of the statute.[6] The Phase II Regulations were an attempt to reduce the regulatory burdens on the health care industry by easing some of the restrictions from the Phase I Regulations.[7] However, CMS

---

3. 66 Fed. Reg. 856 (Jan. 4, 2001).
4. The ABA Health Law Section published a detailed overview of the Phase I Regulations in a special edition of The Health Lawyer.in January 2001. The edition, entitled "Stark II Final Rule—Phase I: A Kinder and Gentler Stark?" describes all aspects of the Phase I Regulations in detail.
5. 69 Fed. Reg. 16,054 (Mar. 26, 2004).
6. Section 1877(b)(4) of the Social Security Act, 42 U.S.C. § 1395nn(b)(4), authorizes the Secretary of HHS to create additional exceptions, or expand existing exceptions, where doing so does not pose a risk of program or patient abuse.
7. The ABA Health Law Section again published a detailed overview of the Phase II Regulations in The Health Lawyer. The second overview, "Stark II—Phase II—The Final Voyage," was published in an April 2004 special edition.

was not done interpreting Stark, and some of the changes would be reversed later. As with all subsequent changes, this round became fully integrated with the previous rounds of regulations to create a unified body of regulations.

4) Stark II, Phase III Regulations

The third round of major regulations under Stark II was issued on September 5, 2007 (the Phase III Regulations).[8] The Phase III Regulations became effective on December 4, 2007, although certain applications of the stand-in-the-shoes rules were delayed by a subsequent rule published on November 15, 2007. The Phase III Regulations again responded to comments raised during the prior phases of the regulations and addressed the entirety of the Stark regulatory scheme then in effect.[9] Within the Preamble to the Phase III Regulations, CMS again stated that the latest regulations were designed to simplify requirements and provide flexibility to those in the health care industry. Despite CMS's goal, the Stark Regulations remain a trap for the unwary and require careful attention to ensure that the relationships that implicate Stark satisfy its requirements to avoid tainting a relationship and potentially resulting in an enforcement action.

5) Subsequent Regulatory Changes

Following the major rounds of regulatory changes identified above, CMS continues to tinker with the Stark Regulations. CMS included important revisions in the 2008 Medicare Physician Fee Schedule final rule,[10] the 2009 Inpatient Prospective Payment System final rule,[11] the 2009 Medicare Physician Fee Schedule final rule,[12] the 2010 Medicare Physician Fee Schedule final rule,[13] the 2011 Hos-

8. 72 Fed. Reg. 51,012 (Sept. 5, 2007).
9. The ABA Health Law Section published a third overview of the Stark Regulations at the time the Phase III regulations were finalized. The third overview, "Stark II Phase III—'The Full Picture'" was published in a special edition of THE HEALTH LAWYER.in September 2007.
10. 72 Fed. Reg. 66,222 (Nov. 27, 2007).
11. 73 Fed. Reg. 38,502 (July 7, 2008).
12. 73 Fed. Reg. 69,726 (Nov. 19, 2008).
13. 74 Fed. Reg. 61,738 (Nov. 25, 2009).

pital Outpatient Prospective Payment System final rule,[14] and the 2012 Hospital Outpatient Prospective Payment System final rule.[15] These regulations all resulted in a change to some piece of the Stark Regulations. Although some of the subsequent amendments were significant, the changes typically were limited to specific provisions of the Stark Regulations as opposed to making wholesale changes. However, the constant revising underscores the need to monitor all regulations promulgated by CMS for potential changes to the Stark Regulations.

B. The Content of the Regulations

The Stark Regulations contain definitions, exceptions, and relationship structures that all interact to enable compliance with the law's requirements. Understanding commonly used definitions and exceptions is necessary to perform an assessment of any Stark issue. Once the key terms are understood, it is possible to understand the terms of use and other phrases that take on special meanings in the context of the Stark Regulations.

1) Key Definitions:
a. Designated Health Services
The most important definition under Stark is designated health services or DHS. This term of art is defined to include: (1) clinical laboratory services; (2) physical therapy, occupational therapy, and outpatient speech-language pathology services; (3) radiology and certain other imaging services; (4) radiation therapy services and supplies; (5) durable medical equipment and supplies; (6) parenteral and enteral nutrients, equipment, and supplies; (7) prosthetics, orthotics, and prosthetic devices and supplies; (8) home health services; (9) outpatient prescription drugs; and (10) inpatient and outpatient hospital services.[16]

---

14. 75 Fed. Reg. 72,240 (Nov. 24, 2010).
15. 76 Fed. Red. 74,517 (Nov. 30, 2011).
16. 42 C.F.R. § 411.351 (Designated health services).

Only the services included in the definition of DHS invoke Stark. For example, services paid under the ambulatory surgery center fee schedule are not designated health services, and thus referrals for such services are outside the purview of Stark. One of the keys to a Stark analysis is determining whether the services to be performed are encompassed with the definition of DHS. If the service being reviewed is not included, a Stark issue probably does not exist.[17]

b. Entity
The term "entity", like many other Stark definitions, is defined broadly to encompass many different types of setups. An entity is "a physician's sole practice or a practice of multiple physicians or any other person, sole proprietorship, public or private agency or trust, corporation, partnership, limited liability company, foundation, nonprofit corporation, or unincorporated association that furnishes DHS."[18]

c. Fair Market Value
Fair market value is another term with a unique definition for purposes of Stark. It is defined as "the value in arm's-length transactions, consistent with the general market value."[19]

General market value is defined as "the price that an asset would bring as the result of bona fide bargaining between well-informed buyers and sellers who are not otherwise in a position to generate business for the other party, or the compensation that would be included in a service agreement as the result of bona fide bargaining between well-informed parties to the agreement who are not otherwise in a position to generate business for the other party, on the date of acquisition of the asset or at the time of the service agreement."[20] An ever-important caveat is that the parties are assumed to not otherwise be in a position to be able to refer business to each other. Excluding the ability to refer business from

17. It is important to note that a financial relationship between a referring physician and an entity that is created through the furnishing of services that are not DHS must still be compliant, lest the relationship create a Stark problem when services that are DHS are furnished by the entity.
18. 42 C.F.R. § 411.351 (Entity).
19. 42 C.F.R. § 411.351 (Fair market value).
20. *Id.*

considerations under Stark is a recurring theme throughout the Stark Regulations.

In the context of space and equipment leases, fair market value is the "value of rental property for general commercial purposes."[21] For purposes of space leases, proximity or convenience to the lessor cannot be considered, if the lessor is a potential source of referrals to the lessee.

The Stark definition of fair market value is different from that typically encountered in a non–health care accounting context. Accordingly, a fair market value assessment that may be acceptable in another industry may not be acceptable when looking at Stark. As such, when assessing the fair market value component of a proposed arrangement, it can often be beneficial to engage an independent health care valuator who has experience working with the unique aspects of the requirements of the Stark Regulations.

It is important to remember that valuing a proposed arrangement is outside the scope of an attorney's duties and obligations. Another appropriate professional should be identified and tasked with conducting a valuation analysis.

d. Physician and Immediate Family Member

A physician includes a doctor of medicine, a doctor of osteopathy, a doctor of dental surgery or dental medicine, a doctor of podiatric medicine, a doctor of optometry, or a chiropractor, as well as a professional corporation of which such physician is the sole owner.[22]

The definition of physician alone is not noteworthy. The extension of prohibited referral relationships to a physician's immediate family members is the factor that can result in surprises. Immediate family members are defined to be a large group of individuals, including the physician's "husband or wife; birth or adoptive parent, child or sibling; stepparent, stepchild, stepbrother, or stepsister; father-in-law, mother-in-law, son-in-law, daughter-in-law, brother-in-law, or sister-in-law; grandparent or grandchild; and spouse of a grandparent, or grandchild."[23] When the definitions of "physician"

---

21. *Id.*
22. 42 C.F.R. § 411.351 (Physician).
23. 42 C.F.R. § 411.351 (Immediate family member of member of a physician's immediate family).

and "immediate family member" are taken together, the number of individuals who could potentially be involved in a Stark-covered relationship becomes very large. As such, an analysis of whether there is a financial relationship with an entity to which the physician refers designated health services must consider more than just the individual physician, but should also be extended to a wide swath of the physician's immediate family. In fact, physician employment agreements sometimes require the employed physician to disclose where their family members work.

e. Referral

A referral is any request, order of, or the certifying or recertifying of the need for any designated health services that is payable by Medicare.[24] Any designated health services personally performed by the referring physician falls outside the definition. A DHS is not personally performed if any other person performs the service including the referring physician's employees, independent contractors, or members of a group practice. A referral may be imputed to the referring physician if such physician directly or indirectly controls a referral made by another provider. However, a request by (1) a pathologist for clinical diagnostic laboratory tests and pathological examination services, (2) a radiologist for diagnostic radiology services, or (3) a radiation oncologist for radiation therapy or ancillary services necessary for and integral to the provision of radiation therapy does not constitute a referral, if (1) the request results from a consultation initiated by another physician and (2) the tests or services are furnished by or under the supervision of the pathologist, radiologist, radiation oncologist, or the corresponding type of physician in the same group practice.

f. Remuneration

The Stark Regulations also contain an expansive definition of remuneration. Remuneration of any type will implicate Stark under a prohibited arrangement. Remuneration is "any payment or other benefit made directly or indirectly, overtly or covertly, in cash or

---

24. 42. C.F.R. § 411.351 (Referral).

in kind."[25] Certain exchanges are carved out of the definition, but essentially remuneration is broadly defined to include any transfer or exchange of a benefit. Cash is not required; any exchange of financial or similar benefit will qualify.

g. Rural Area

A rural area is an area that does not constitute an urban area.[26] An urban area is a Metropolitan Statistical Area (MSA) or New England County Metropolitan Area (NECMA), as defined by the Executive Office of Management and Budget;[27] or certain specified counties in New England.[28]

h. Set in Advance

Many of the exceptions require compensation to be set in advance. Compensation satisfies this requirement if the aggregate amount, which can be a time-based, per-unit-of-service-based amount, or other formulaic approach, is set out in an agreement between the parties prior to the service or item being furnished.[29] The Stark Regulations require compensation to be set and not constantly changing, thus giving predictability. When compensation is allowed to fluctuate there is a concern that any movement is done to reflect volume or value of referrals.

If a formula is used, the formula as detailed in the agreement must contain enough detail that it can be objectively verified. The formula may not be altered during the course of the arrangement in such a way that the volume or value of referrals or other business generated between the parties is taken into account.

In the 2009 Inpatient Prospective Payment System final rule, CMS clarified that the compensation terms or rental charges may be amended during the term of an agreement.[30] CMS conditioned the ability of parties to make mid-term amendments on: (1) the arrange-

---

25. 42 C.F.R. § 411.351 (Remuneration).
26. 42 C.F.R. § 411.351 (Rural area).
27. The Executive Office of Management and Budget updates the areas at least annually. Information about what falls into a given MSA or NECMA can be found on the Executive Office of Management and Budget's website: http://www.whitehouse.gov/omb.
28. 42 C.F.R. § 412.62(f)(1)(ii).
29. 42 C.F.R. § 411.354(d)(1).
30. 73 Fed. Reg. 48697 (Aug. 19, 2008).

ment still satisfying an applicable exception, (2) the amended compensation or rent being determined before the amendment goes into effect, (3) the formula for the amended compensation or rent not taking into account the volume or value of referrals or other business generated, and (4) the amended compensation or rent terms remaining in place for at least one year from the date of the amendment.[31] This procedure applies to arrangements that are structured to meet an exception that requires a one-year term, such as the exception for personal services arrangements and the exceptions for space and equipment rentals. The fair market value exception does not fall into this category.

2) Nature of Financial Relationships

The Stark Regulations subdivide financial relationships, both ownership and compensation, into direct and indirect financial relationships.[32] It is important to understand the implications of each to assess appropriately the nature of a proposed arrangement.

a. Direct Financial Relationships

A direct financial relationship exists if remuneration passes directly between the referring physician and the "entity furnishing DHS without any intervening persons or entities."[33] The definition remains the same regardless of whether the relationship is one of ownership or investment or one of compensation.[34]

When considering a family of corporate entities, an ownership or investment interest in a subsidiary company is not a direct financial relationship with the parent company or any other subsidiary company in the corporate structure.[35] However, a direct financial

---

31. *Id.* As a practical matter, the amended compensation must be *scheduled* to remain in effect for a year and not actually last for a year. This circumstance can arise because the parties may amend the compensation terms of an agreement mid-term and then, before a year has passed, amend the terms again.

32. 42 C.F.R. § 411.354(a).

33. *Id.* at § 411.354(a)(2).

34. *Id.*

35. *Id.* at § 411.354(b)(2). However, if the subsidiary itself has an ownership or investment interest in the parent or other subsidiaries, this exception does not apply and this type of relationship can still be an indirect financial relationship and must be evaluated accordingly. *Id.*

relationship would be present if the subsidiary company itself has an ownership or investment interest in the parent or another subsidiary.

Further, various specific ownership and investment interests are not included in the definition of direct financial relationships.[36] For example, an interest arising from a retirement plan, stock options and convertible securities prior to exercise or conversion, an unsecured loan that is subordinated to a credit facility, an "under arrangements" contract, or a security interest in equipment sold by a physician to a hospital are not ownership and investment interests that create a direct financial relationship.[37]

b. Indirect Financial Relationships

An indirect ownership or investment interest exists if, between the referring physician and the entity furnishing designated health services, there exists an unbroken chain of any number of persons or entities, but no less than one, having an ownership or investment interest between them.[38] The entity furnishing designated health services need not know the precise composition of the chain in order to create the indirect relationship.[39]

For indirect compensation arrangements, although the unbroken chain element is still present, the overall analysis becomes more complicated. An indirect compensation arrangement exists if: (1) there is an unbroken chain of any number of (but not less than one) financial relationships between the referring physician and the entity furnishing DHS; (2) the referring physician receives aggregate compensation from the person or entity with which the physician has a *direct* financial relationship that varies with or otherwise reflects the volume or value of referrals or other business generated by the referring physician; and (3) the entity furnishing DHS has actual knowledge of, or acts in reckless disregard or deliberate ignorance of the fact that the referring physician receives aggregate compensation that varies with or otherwise reflects the value or

---

36. *Id.* at § 411.354(b)(3).
37. *Id.*
38. *Id.* at § 411.354(b)(5)(i)(A).
39. *Id.* at § 411.354(b)(5)(ii).

volume of referrals or other business generated by the referring physician for the entity furnishing the DHS.[40]

c. Stand in the Shoes—A Hybrid Analysis

Where applicable, the stand-in-the-shoes (SITS) principle transforms an otherwise indirect financial relationship into a direct financial relationship.[41] A physician owner of his or her physician organization is considered to be standing in the shoes of his or her physician organization and is deemed to have the same compensation arrangement that his or her physician organization has with the DHS entity and on the same terms. SITS allows for only one level of analysis and removes the need to perform what may be a complicated indirect financial relationship analysis. According to commentary published by CMS, SITS focuses upon one arrangement, instead of trying to determine if each arrangement satisfies Stark.

For example, where a physician group practice has an agreement with a hospital to provide emergency call services, each owner of the group practice will be deemed to have the same arrangement with the hospital as is set forth in the agreement between the group practice and the hospital. If there is a problem with the agreement between the group practice and the hospital, e.g., the compensation under the agreement is not fair market value, each physician owner of the group practice will have a non-conforming compensation arrangement with the hospital and each owner physician's referrals for designated health services to the hospital during the period of non-compliance of the agreement will be tainted. Non-owner physicians in the group practice would not be tagged with that relationship. Instead, one would have to analyze whether the non-owner physicians would have an indirect compensation arrangement with the entity furnishing the designated health services based on an

---

40. *Id.* at § 411.354(c)(2). If the financial relationship between the physician (or immediate family member) and the person or entity in the chain with which the referring physician (or immediate family member) has a direct financial relationship is an ownership or investment interest, the determination of whether the aggregate compensation varies with or otherwise reflects the volume or value of referrals or other business generated by the referring physician will be measured by the non-ownership or non-investment interest closest in the chain to the referring physician (or immediate family member). *Id.* at § 411.354(c)(2)(ii).
41. 42 C.F.R. § 411.354(c)(2)(iv).

unbroken chain of financial relationships that would run physician to group practice (compensation arrangement) to hospital (compensation arrangement), and, if so, whether that indirect compensation could meet an exception.

Note that only "true" owners of a physician organization are required to stand in the shoes of their physician organization. Nominal or titular physician owners, such as the physician owner holding title to stock in a friendly professional corporation in a state with a corporate practice of medicine prohibition, are not required to stand in the shoes of their physician organization. The parties may voluntarily elect to treat such an owner or other physician non-owner as standing in the shoes of the physician organization though. Note also, that a physician and his or her solely owned professional corporation are treated as one and the same. That is, even before the stand-in-the-shoes principle was finalized, a physician and his or her solely owned professional corporation were considered one and the same, so that a physician was deemed to have the same financial relationship with a DHS entity that his or her solely owned professional corporation had with that DHS entity.

It is important to remember that SITS only applies to physicians. CMS has proposed, but did not finalize an analogous stand-in-the-shoes principle for entities. Accordingly, SITS is relevant only when considering the physician side of an arrangement.

3) Key Exceptions

Although Stark generally prohibits a physician from referring designated health services to an entity with which the physician (or his or her immediate family member) has a financial relationship, there are numerous exceptions that enable relationships to be formed and referrals to be made. Because Stark is a strict liability statute, it is essential to meet every element of an exception. Failure to comply with all of the elements of an exception will mean that exception is not available, and if there is a prohibited financial relationship that does not satisfy any exception, any referral of designated health services to an entity with which the physician has the prohibited financial relationship will result in a violation. The exceptions to Stark can be broken into three main categories: (1) those that protect services performed under certain circumstances, (2) those that protect ownership or investment interests, and (3) those that protect compensation arrangements.

a. Service-Based Exceptions

As the category implies, the service-based exceptions protect certain services that are performed under certain conditions, without regard to the nature of the financial relationship between the referring physician and the entity. If the requirements of an exception are satisfied, the prohibition on referrals does not apply. Of course, although the financial relationship between the referring physician and the entity is disregarded in examining whether the service-based exception is met, the financial relationship must be considered to the extent that the referring physician refers other designated health services to the entity that is not protected by a services-based exception. Where the referring physician has an ownership interest in the entity, if a service-based exception cannot be met, it will be very difficult to find an applicable ownership/investment exception.

i. Physician Services

Physician services payable by Medicare are exempt, if furnished personally by another physician who is a member of the referring physician's group practice, or under the supervision of another physician who is a member of the group practice.[42] A group practice is a single legal entity operated primarily for the purpose of being a physician group practice and may be owned or organized by a combination of parties, including physicians, other health care facilities, or other persons or entities; but at least two physicians must be members of the group.[43] A multi-specialty group practice is likely to satisfy this exception, which can allow for the referral of patients within the group for its various practice areas. Awareness of this exception may be helpful as instances are beginning to occur more frequently where it can be utilized. For instance, in a multi-specialty group practice setting where a radiologist is part of the group practice and will provide the professional component

---

42. 42 C.F.R. § 411.355(a).
43. 42 C.F.R. § 411.352. There are many components to the definition of a "group practice."

of a service, i.e., reading an image, when a patient is referred to the radiologist by another member of the radiologist's group practice the physician services exception may be satisfied.

ii. In-Office Ancillary Services

The in-office ancillary services (IOAS) exception is perhaps the most important Stark exception. Whereas the IOAS exception can provide broad protection, arrangements must be structured and operated carefully to satisfy its elements. The elements of the IOAS exception can be broken into three main categories: (1) the individual performing the DHS, (2) the location where the DHS is performed, and (3) who bills the DHS.[44]

Under the IOAS exception, the services must be furnished personally by (1) the referring physician, i.e., self-performed, (2) a physician who is a member of the same group practice as the referring physician, or (3) an individual who is supervised by either the referring physician or another physician in the group practice. If supervision is relied upon to satisfy the IOAS exception performance element, the appropriate level of supervision must be used. Although the statute uses the language "directly supervised," which may appear to be referring to direct supervision, CMS takes the position that whatever level of supervision is required under the Medicare payment rules is the level of supervision required for purposes of the IOAS exception.[45]

For the location element, the designated health services must be furnished in (1) the same building where the referring physician or another member of the group practice regularly practices,[46] (2) in a centralized building that is used by the referring physician or the group practice for some or all of its clinical laboratory services, or (3) a centralized building that is used by the referring physician or the group practice for some or all of the group's DHS. When considering the location where services under the IOAS exception can be

---

44. 42 C.F.R. § 411.355(b).

45. 42 C.F.R. § 410.32 defines the three levels of supervision (general, direct, and personal), and specifies the supervision level required for certain diagnostic tests. The required supervision level for other diagnostic tests and for therapeutic services is set forth in other regulations, manual instructions, and on CMS's website.

46. The requirements for meeting the "same building" test are somewhat involved and are set forth in three alternative sets of criteria at 42 C.F.R. § 411.355(b)(2)(i).

performed, both types of buildings, same or centralized, are given special definitions by the Stark Regulations. A centralized building is all or part of a building (including a mobile trailer, van, or vehicle) that is owned or leased by the group practice full-time, i.e., no time-sharing occurs, and is used exclusively by the group practice.[47] The "same building" is a structure or combination of structures sharing a single postal street address, but does not include mobile trailers, vans, or vehicles as is permissible under the centralized building definition.[48] This means that a service will not meet the IOAS exception if it needs to be performed in a location that cannot meet either the centralized building or same building definition. For example, a group practice could own a subsidiary entity to perform imaging or provide medical equipment, but cannot use the IOAS exception if those services are not offered in an appropriate location.

Lastly, the designated health services must be billed by (1) the physician performing or supervising the service, (2) the group practice of which the performing or supervising physician is a member, (3) the group practice if the supervising physician is a "physician in the group practice" as that phrase is defined in 42 C.F.R. § 411.351, (4) an entity wholly owned by the performing or supervising physician or such physician's group practice, or (5) an independent third-party billing company acting as an agent for one of the foregoing. The billing aspect of the IOAS exception may be the easiest to satisfy. Billing arrangements are often set in an employment agreement or similar agreement.

Special rules also exist for home care physicians under the IOAS exception.[49] For a referring physician who principally treats patients in the patient's private home, the same building requirement is met if the referring physician, or a qualified person accompanying the referring physician, provides the designated health services contemporaneously with a physician service that is not DHS in the patient's home. A private home does not include a nursing, long-term care, or other facility or institution, though a patient may have a private home in such a place.

---

47. 42 C.F.R. § 411.351 (Centralized building).
48. 42 C.F.R. § 411.351 (Same building).
49. 42 C.F.R. § 411.355(b)(6).

The Affordable Care Act added another requirement for certain imaging services.[50] For magnetic resonance imaging, computed tomography, and positron emission tomography services, the referring physician must provide written notice to the patient at the time of the referral that the patient may receive such imaging services from another physician or supplier. The written notice must include a list of at least five other suppliers that provide the service within a twenty-five-mile radius of the referring physician's office, which suppliers can provide the service at the time of the referral. If there are fewer than five such suppliers, then the list must include all suppliers within the twenty-five-mile radius of the referring physician's office.

Finally, it should be noted that whereas the IOAS exception protects the great majority of designated health services referred within a group practice, it cannot be used for most durable medical equipment (DME). The DME that can be protected by the IOAS exception are limited to canes, crutches, walkers, folding manual wheelchairs, blood glucose monitors that meet certain conditions,[51] and certain infusion pumps.[52]

iii. Academic Medical Centers
The third service-based exception relates to academic medical centers (AMC).[53] Given the prevalence of AMCs in many areas of the country, understanding this exception can be useful.

The exception for AMCs exempts services if requirements regarding the physicians involved and the AMC itself are met. The referring physician must meet the following criteria: (1) be a bona fide employee of a component of the AMC, (2) be licensed to practice medicine in the state where the physician practices medicine (a license is typically necessary for a physician to practice medicine), (3) have a bona fide faculty appointment at the medical school affiliated with the AMC, and (4) provide either substantial academic or clinical teaching services for which the physician receives compensation. The compensation paid to the physician must be set in

---

50. 42 C.F.R. § 411.355(b)(7).
51. 42 C.F.R. § 411.355(b)(4).
52. 42 C.F.R. § 411.355.
53. 42 C.F.R. § 411.355(e).

advance for fair market value, and must not take into account the volume or value of referrals or other business generated by the referring physician within the AMC. The elements relating to compensation are very standard and reflect the requirements of many of the compensation exceptions explained later in this chapter. However, controversy can arise over what constitutes fair market value compensation, which compensation should be for services actually rendered.[54]

The AMC must meet the following three conditions: (1) transfers between components of the AMC must support the mission(s) of the AMC, (2) the relationships between the components of the AMC must be set forth in written agreements or some other form of writing adopted by the governing body of each component, and (3) all money paid to a physician for research must be used to support bona fide research or teaching.

iv. Intra-Family Rural Referrals

In the rural setting, it may be possible to exempt services rendered following a referral from a referring physician to an immediate family member or entity with which an immediate family member has a financial relationship.[55] To qualify for the exception: (1) the referred patient must reside in a rural area, (2) no other person or entity is available to provide the services in a timely manner within twenty-five miles or forty-five minutes' transportation time from the patient's residence, (3) no other person or entity is available to timely provide the services where the patient resides, and (4) the financial relationship does not violate the Anti-Kickback Statute or any other federal or state law governing billing or claims submission. The referring physician or the physician's immediate family member must make inquiries to determine if any other person or

---

54. A detailed analysis of the AMC exception was performed by the United States District Court for the Western District of Kentucky in the case of *U.S. ex rel. Villafane v. Solinger*, 543 F. Supp. 2d 678 (W.D. Ky. 2008), which is summarized in chapter 3, Section C. As is explained in Chapter 3, Stark practitioners question the usefulness of court opinions given the often imprecise or bad factual records and sometimes questionable analysis of Stark.
55. 42 C.F.R. § 411.355(j).

entity is available to provide the service within the parameters set by condition (2).

It should be noted that the Intra-Family Rural Referral exception applies to where the DHS is provided and is based on where the patient resides. Accordingly, it is theoretically possible for urban providers to take advantage of this exception.

b. Ownership/Investment Interest Exceptions

The ownership and investment interest exceptions protect ownership or investment interests in entities.[56] The excepted interests can arise through publicly traded securities or mutual funds. The discussion of these exceptions will focus on rural providers and hospital ownership. These two ownership or investment exceptions were greatly impacted by passage of the Patient Protection and Affordable Care Act (the Affordable Care Act) in 2010 and by the resulting implementing regulations.

i. Rural Provider Exception

Ownership or investment interests are permissible in a rural provider that furnishes designated health services in a rural area, as that term is defined in the regulations.[57] A rural provider is an entity that furnishes at least 75 percent of its designated health services to residents of a rural area.

ii. Hospital Ownership

Ownership of a whole hospital provides another exception from the Stark referral and billing prohibitions.[58] The so-called "whole hospital" exception requires: (1) the referring physician to be authorized to perform services at the hospital; (2) the hospital to not be a specialty hospital for the period December 8, 2003, through June 8, 2005; and (3) the ownership or investment interest to be in the entire hospital, not just a distinct part or department of the hospital, i.e., the whole hospital, not just a line of service.

---

56. 42 C.F.R. § 411.356.
57. 42 C.F.R. § 411.356(c)(1). See Section B.1.g. for the definition of rural area.
58. 42 C.F.R. § 411.356(c)(3).

iii. Impact of the Affordable Care Act on Rural Provider and Hospital Ownership Exceptions

The Affordable Care Act significantly changed the requirements by which a hospital can qualify for either the rural provider or hospital ownership exceptions.[59] Greater reporting to CMS and more transparency are just a part of the changes. The changes made by the Affordable Care Act to the statutory elements of the exceptions are[60]:

- Physician ownership or investment in the hospital existed on December 31, 2010, and a Medicare provider agreement was in place;
- The number of licensed operating rooms, procedure rooms and beds cannot be increased from what existed as of March 23, 2010;
- The hospital must annually provide reports to the secretary of HHS concerning the identity of each physician owner or investor in the hospital along with the nature and extent of the ownership or investment interest;
- The hospital must have procedures in place requiring any referring physician who is an owner or investor in the hospital to disclose to patients the nature of that physician's ownership or investment interest with enough advance notice to allow the patient to make a meaningful decision about the receipt of care;
- The hospital does not condition a physician's ownership or investment interest on making or influencing referrals to the hospital;
- The hospital discloses the physician ownership or investment interests on its public website or in any public advertisement;
- To ensure bona fide investment in the hospital: (1) the percentage of the total value of ownership or investment interests held by physicians in the aggregate does not exceed

---

59. Section 6001 of the Affordable Care Act, Pub. L. No. 111-148 (codified at 42 U.S.C. § 1395nn(i)).
60. The changes enacted by the Affordable Care Act were codified at 42 U.S.C. § 1395nn(i) (1)(A-F).

such percentage as of March 23, 2010, (2) ownership or investment interests are not offered to physicians on more favorable terms than non-physicians, (3) the hospital does not, directly or indirectly, provide loans or financing for any investment in the hospital by a physician owner or investor, (4) the hospital does not, directly or indirectly, guarantee a loan, make a loan payment, or otherwise subsidize a loan of any physician or group of physicians related to the acquisition of an ownership or investment interest in the hospital, (5) returns are distributed to each owner or investor in an amount that is directly proportional to the ownership or investment interest (no favoritism), (6) physician owners and investors do not receive, directly or indirectly, guaranteed receipt of or a right to acquire any other business interests related to the hospital, and (7) physician owners or investors are not afforded the opportunity to purchase or lease any property controlled by the hospital on terms more favorable than offered to non-physician owners or investors;

- If the hospital admits a patient and does not have any physician available on hospital premises to provide services during all hours when the hospital is providing services to the patient, then the hospital must disclose such information to the patient and receive a signed acknowledgement of such from the patient before the patient may be admitted. The hospital must also have the capacity to provide assessment and initial treatment for patients and refer and transfer patients to hospitals that can treat the needs of patients; and
- The hospital cannot have been converted from an ambulatory surgical center into a hospital on or after March 23, 2010.

The Affordable Care Act obligates the secretary of HHS to annually publish, on CMS's website, the information submitted by hospitals concerning the identity of each physician owner or investor along with the nature and extent of each such physician's ownership or investment interest.[61] This public display of information is

---

61. 42 U.S.C. § 1395nn(i)(2).

part of an effort to create more transparency overall in provider relationships.

The list of changes resulting from the Affordable Care Act included that a hospital could not expand. However, an exception was included. The secretary of HHS was permitted to establish an expansion process through the regulatory process, which would include the opportunity for community input. The regulations establishing the expansion exception were included in the 2012 Hospital Outpatient Prospective Payment System Final Rule.[62] Generally, hospitals are eligible to submit an application for expansion once every two years from the date of CMS's decision on the hospital's most recent application.[63] The procedure itself requires submission of a written request, by mail or electronically, to CMS to qualify for the exception, along with certain documentation and a certification that all information is true and correct.[64] The hospital must publicly disclose its expansion request until CMS makes a decision. Additionally, interested individuals and/or entities within the hospital's community may provide input to CMS on the proposed expansion.

The criteria for the submission depend upon whether the hospital is an applicable hospital or a high Medicaid facility. An applicable hospital must[65]: (1) be located in a county that has a percentage population increase that is at least 150 percent of the percentage population increase in the state where the hospital is located during the most recent five-year period, (2) have its percentage of annual Medicaid inpatient admissions be equal to or greater than the average percentage of such admissions for all other hospitals in the county during the most recent fiscal year, (3) not discriminate against beneficiaries of federal health care programs, (4) be located in a state in which the average bed capacity in the state is less than the national average bed capacity, and (5) have an average bed occupancy rate that is greater than the average bed occupancy rate in the state where the hospital is located during the most recent fiscal year.

---

62. 76 Fed. Reg. 74122 (Nov. 30, 2011). The expansion regulations can be found encoded at 42 C.F.R. § 411.362(c) (2011).
63. 42 C.F.R. § 411.362(c)(1).
64. 42 C.F.R. § 411.362(c)(4).
65. 42 C.F.R. § 411.362(c)(2).

A high Medicaid facility must meet different criteria, which are as follows[66]: (1) the hospital does not need to be the sole hospital in its area, (2) the hospital's percentage of total inpatient admissions of Medicaid patients must be greater than the percentage of such admissions by any other hospital in the same area in each of the previous three years, and (3) the hospital does not discriminate against beneficiaries of federal health care programs.

The changes to the rural provider and whole hospital exception can be expected to impact a large number of providers. Despite the often-disproportionate focus on urban areas, there are still a large number of rural areas in the country where these exceptions will need to be examined and used.

c. Compensation Arrangement Exceptions

The compensation-based exceptions are all grouped at 42 C.F.R. § 411.357. These exceptions contribute to the bulk of the available exceptions to Stark. Understanding the elements and uses of the compensation-based exceptions is very important to any attorney working with Stark. The exceptions discussed in this section are only a portion of the compensation exceptions set forth at 42 C.F.R. § 411.357. When analyzing an arrangement, it is always necessary to consider all of the available compensation exceptions.

i. Exceptions for Renting Office Space and Equipment

The two exceptions for rentals—office space and equipment—are largely identical, aside from the subject matter of the two exceptions.[67] Rentals (or leases) may be exempt from Stark if: (1) the agreement is set forth in a writing signed by the parties that specifies the premises or equipment covered; (2) the agreement has a term of at least one year; (3) the amount of space or equipment rented is reasonable and necessary for a legitimate business purpose and is used exclusively by the lessee when the lessee is using the space or equipment; (4) the amount of the rental charge is set in advance at fair market value; (5) the rental charge is not determined in a manner that takes into account the volume or value of

---

66. 42 C.F.R. § 411.362(c)(3).
67. 42 C.F.R. § 411.357(a), (b).

referrals or other business generated between the parties or using a formula that relates to a percentage of revenue or per-click uses; and (6) the agreement is commercially reasonable. There is also a month-to-month holdover period for up to six months, if a lease is not immediately renewed.

The lease exceptions provide a prime example of the continually evolving nature of the Stark Regulations. Previously, per-click, or unit of service, arrangements were permissible with regard to rental agreements. This meant that a rental amount could be tied to the actual use of the space or equipment. However, CMS altered the two exceptions in the 2009 Inpatient Prospective Payment Systems final rule. After the effective date of the amendment (which was delayed for one year), per-click arrangements became prohibited insofar as the lessor would receive a per-click payment for use of the space or equipment by the lessee in furnishing services referred by the lessor to the lessee. This change necessitated a review of all rental agreements then existing to ensure that a previously permissible arrangement did not remain in place and cause a violation going forward.

Partial or time-share rentals are permissible. However, extra care should be used in preparing such a rental. If a lessee does not always use the space or equipment, the arrangement can raise the government's suspicion of fraud or other improper purpose. In particular, the schedule of use and rent should clearly reflect the partial use and be fair in light of such partial use. The schedule, i.e., days and/or hours of use, should ideally be set forth in the rental agreement before the space or equipment is used and not be determined on an ad hoc basis. The lessee should also only pay the pro rata share of rent attributable to actual use, which should also include the partial use of common areas.

ii. Bona Fide Employment Relationship

The exception for a "bona fide employment relationship" protects referrals from a physician (or immediate family member of the physician) who is an employee of an entity, such as a group practice or hospital. The exception requires that: (1) the employment be for identifiable services; (2) the remuneration paid be consistent with the fair market value of the services; and (3) the remuneration would be commercially reasonable even if no referrals were made by the employee to the employer.[68] It is possible to provide productivity bonuses, but such bonuses must be based upon services personally performed by the physician or the physician's immediate family member.

It is interesting to note that the bona fide employment relationship exception does not require the arrangement to be in writing and signed. The lack of a signed writing requirement is fairly unique among the Stark exceptions and occasionally may be able to save an arrangement that at first appears to be in violation of Stark because a written or signed agreement is missing. However, it is still recommended, and a best practice, that all employment agreements be in writing and signed.

iii. Personal Service Arrangements

The exception for personal service arrangements complements the bona fide employment exception by protecting arrangements involving independent contractor physicians.[69] Under a typical arrangement between a physician and an entity, the physician would provide certain, specified services, such as medical director services or emergency room call. This exception can be used for clinical, administrative, or any other type of services.

The exception requires the following elements be met: (1) each arrangement involving the parties is set forth in writing signed by the parties and states the services to be provided; (2) the arrangement covers all of the services to be rendered; (3) the aggregate services to be provided do not exceed what is reasonable and necessary for legitimate business purposes; (4) each arrangement lasts for at least one year; (5) the compensation to be paid is set in advance for fair market value without taking into account the volume or value of any referrals or other business generated between the parties; and (6) the services do not involve the counseling or promotion of any activity that violates any federal or state law. The personal service arrangements exception, like the rental exceptions, protects a holdover from the arrangement for up to six months, provided that the terms of the underlying arrangement do not change.

---

68. 42 C.F.R. § 411.357(c).
69. 42 C.F.R. § 411.357(d).

As stated above, personal service arrangements are often used when physicians are hired to be medical directors. As a medical director, the physician ordinarily plays more of an administrative, oversight role and will often maintain his or her own medical practice, thus presenting the opportunity for referrals of designated health services to the entity and the need to meet an exception to Stark.

The medical directorship example can highlight the need to consider carefully the fair market value compensation and reasonable services elements of the personal service arrangement exception. A medical director should be compensated only for the services actually provided. The position should not be used as a means of directing extra funds to the physician with the expectation of referrals coming back. Additionally, the time spent on the medical director role should be tracked to verify whether the parties reasonably estimated the time needed. Another consideration is whether the position is even needed and what the actual purpose is for retaining the provider as a medical director. One indication that the services of the position are not needed as required by the exception could be an excessive number of medical directors retained by an entity.

iv. Physician Recruitment

Another common activity engaged in by the health care industry is the recruitment of physicians. Just as in other industries, health care entities want to offer incentives to encourage a physician to join the practice or organization. The physician recruitment exception enables a hospital[70] to offer remuneration to a physician, such as a guaranteed income loan, with the intention of inducing the physician to relocate to the geographic area served by the hospital to join the hospital's medical staff.[71] To qualify for the exception, the arrangement must: (1) be in writing signed by the parties; (2) not

---

70. The recruitment exception is also available to rural health clinics and federally qualified health centers ("FQHC"), but to no other health care entities, such as physician practices. For ease of reference, "hospital" is used instead of "hospital or rural health clinic of FQHC."

71. 42 C.F.R. § 411.357(e). Generally, the physician must relocate to the hospital's geographical service area from outside of the hospital's geographical service area at a distance of 25 miles or greater. The relocation requirement does not apply to graduating residents or physicians in practice for less than one year.

be conditioned on the physician referring patients to the hospital; (3) not determine the remuneration paid to the physician in a manner that takes into account the volume or value of referrals or other business generated between the parties; and (4) permit the physician to receive staff privileges and refer business to any other entity except as properly limited under an employment or services contract.

The exception carefully defines what constitutes the geographic area served by the hospital and what it means for a physician to relocate his or her practice. The geographic area of the hospital consists of the smallest number of contiguous zip codes from which the hospital draws at least 75 percent of its inpatients. This may result in the inclusion of zip codes from which the hospital does not actually draw any inpatients. If at least 75 percent of a hospital's patients cannot be identified from all of the contiguous zip codes from which inpatients are drawn, then the geographic service area of the hospital will consist of all contiguous zip codes.

It is permissible for recruitment payments to be made through a group practice[72] and not directly to the physician.[73] If payments are directed through a group practice, the group practice must be a party to the signed agreement. Careful attention should be paid to any income guarantees made to a recruited physician in this context as well. Further, complications can arise if either the group practice or the hospital guarantees any loans made to a physician, in particular if the physician leaves prior to satisfaction of the loan.

v. Isolated Transactions

The isolated transactions exception can play a large role in the sale of a medical practice or other one-time transactions.[74] A transaction satisfies the exception if: (1) the remuneration under the transaction is for fair market value without taking into account the volume or value of referrals or other business generated between the parties; (2) the remuneration is commercially reasonable even if no referrals

---

72. For purposes of the recruitment exception, "group practice" is any physician practice, regardless of whether it meets the definition of group practice set forth at 42 C.F.R. § 411.352.
73. 42 C.F.R. § 411.357(e)(4).
74. 42 C.F.R. § 411.357(f).

were made; and (3) the parties do not engage in any other transactions for six months, except for transactions that meet a Stark exception or commercially reasonable post-closing adjustments.

Although this exception sets forth the basis for the elements of isolated transaction, it is also important to remember that the Stark Regulations contain a specific definition of "transaction."[75] For purposes of Stark, a transaction is an instance or process of two or more persons or entities doing business. An isolated financial transaction can involve either a single payment or installment payments. If installment payments are used, the following elements must be present: (1) the total aggregate payment is set prior to the first payment being made and does not take into account, directly or indirectly, the volume or value of referrals or other business generated by the referring physician, and (2) the payments are immediately negotiable or are guaranteed by a third party, or secured by a negotiable promissory note, or subject to a similar mechanism.

The carve-out for additional transactions that meet another exception to Stark allows for the consummation of multiple, connected agreements. For example, consider what happens when an independent physician practice is sold to a hospital. The practice and its physical assets need to be sold, which is the portion of the transaction likely to fall under the isolated transaction exception. However, how can the physicians from the practice stay connected to the hospital? The hospital could choose to directly employ the physicians, which would fall under the bona fide employment exception; the hospital could arrange for the physicians to provide certain services, which would likely fall under the personal service arrangements exception; or any other arrangement desired by the parties could be structured that meet an exception. The isolated transaction exception primarily helps with the sale because the sale would otherwise be unlikely to fit into another exception under Stark.

vi. Fair Market Value Compensation
The fair market value exception is another Stark exception with potentially broad application.[76] It is also very similar to the per-

---

75. 42 C.F.R. § 411.351 (Transaction).
76. 42 C.F.R. § 411.357(l).

sonal service arrangements exception in practice. The exception often catches compensation arrangements that do not squarely fit into another exception and renders such arrangements permissible. This catchall quality to the fair market value exception makes it very useful.

The fair market value exception requires that an arrangement: (1) is in writing signed by the parties and specifies the items or services covered; (2) sets the timeframe of the arrangement, provided that the terms do not change within any one-year period; (3) specifies the compensation to be provided, which must be set in advance for fair market value without taking into account the volume or value of referrals or other business generated between the parties; (4) is commercially reasonable and furthers legitimate business purposes; (5) does not violate the Anti-Kickback Statute or any other law or regulation relating to billing or claims submission; and (6) does not promote or counsel any activity that violates any federal or state law. The exception specifically excludes space rentals from its coverage, requiring such rentals to meet the specific exception for space rentals.

vii. Indirect Compensation Arrangements

The exception for indirect compensation arrangements protects referrals from a physician who has an indirect compensation arrangement with an entity as defined at 42 C.F.R. § 411.354, which is set forth in Section 2 of this chapter, from violating Stark.[77]

The exception for indirect compensation arrangements requires that (1) the compensation received by the referring physician from the entity with which the physician has a direct compensation arrangement is fair market value for the services and items actually provided without taking the volume or value of referrals or other business generated into account; (2) the arrangement is set out in writing, signed by the parties,[78] and specifies the services covered; and (3) the arrangement does not violate the Anti-Kickback Statute or any other federal or state law related to billing

---

77. 42 C.F.R. §411.357(p).
78. A written agreement is not required if the physician is an employee of the entity with which he or she has a direct compensation arrangement.

or claims submission. The exception requires a written agreement between the physician and the entity with which the physician has a direct compensation arrangement, unless the nature of the direct compensation arrangement is an employer-employee relationship.

viii. Other Compensation Exceptions

As stated at the beginning of this section, the above list of compensation exceptions is only a partial list of the most commonly used compensation exceptions. It is important to remember that other compensation exceptions exist, including:

- Certain arrangements with hospitals;[79]
- Group practice arrangements with a hospital;[80]
- Payments by a physician;[81]
- Charitable donations by a physician;[82]
- Nonmonetary compensation;[83]
- Medical staff incidental benefits;[84]
- Risk-sharing arrangements;[85]
- Compliance training;[86]
- Referral services;[87]
- Obstetrical malpractice insurance subsidies;[88]
- Professional courtesy;[89]
- Retention payments in underserved areas;[90]
- Community-wide health information systems;[91]
- Electronic prescribing items and services;[92] and
- Electronic health records items and services.[93]

---

79. 42 C.F.R. § 411.357(g).
80. 42 C.F.R. § 411.357(h).
81. 42 C.F.R. § 411.357(i).
82. 42 C.F.R. § 411.357(j).
83. 42 C.F.R. § 411.357(k).
84. 42 C.F.R. § 411.357(m).
85. 42 C.F.R. § 411.357(n).
86. 42 C.F.R. § 411.357(o).
87. 42 C.F.R. § 411.357(q).
88. 42 C.F.R. § 411.357(r).
89. 42 C.F.R. § 411.357(s).
90. 42 C.F.R. § 411.357(t).
91. 42 C.F.R. § 411.357(u).
92. 42 C.F.R. § 411.357(v).
93. 42 C.F.R. § 411.357(w).

4) Conclusion

As the summary of a portion of the exceptions to Stark demonstrates, there are a myriad of considerations when entering into an arrangement where the parties have a financial relationship and could be referring designated health services. Further, the attention to detail cannot be ignored, even after an arrangement is memorialized in an agreement. To the contrary, it is necessary to keep monitoring developments involving the Stark Regulations for changes that could impact an arrangement going forward. Even without potential changes to the Stark Regulations, arrangements should be tracked to avoid, among other things, termination of the agreement or non-compliance with agreed-upon terms.[94]

The attorney's role in monitoring may differ depending upon the nature of the attorney's practice. An in-house attorney may be directly responsible for monitoring all arrangements and ensuring that such arrangements remain compliant. An attorney in private practice may need to keep clients up to date on changes and suggest that a review occur, or may be tasked with monitoring responsibilities by a client.

---

94. Outside counsel can alert clients to changes in Stark, whereas in-house counsel may be directly responsible for tracking and monitoring changes.

Interpretations of the Stark Law 3

The Stark Law is difficult both to understand and to comply with in the real world. Commentators have described the Stark Law "in the following ways: 'confusing,' 'complicated,' 'over-reaching, too complex and intrusive;' 'out of synch with managed care' and therefore 'antiquated;' 'chilling' legitimate business; ambiguous . . . requiring 'institutions and physician practices to undertake an exhausting internal . . . evaluation that may—even with the best of intentions and efforts—be extremely difficult to do right;' . . . [t]he Stark labyrinth, [is a] twisted knot of fraud and abuse legislation . . . where the language is so incomprehensible that regulators themselves have trouble understanding it, let alone enforcing it, [and i]n attempting to account for everything—all the exceptions and loopholes and safe harbors—the law actually ends up meaning nothing;' . . . 'the Stark laws are strict and technical, [with] so many elements that can trip you up [and requirements that are] impossible to meet"[1] Therefore, it is not surprising that attempts at interpreting Stark result in confusion and avoidance.

The complexity of Stark is aggravated by the paucity of available interpretations. CMS has produced guidance and interpretations over time, but the material from CMS can be conflicting as CMS's views evolve and change. Few courts have tackled Stark and its many regulations. The handful of courts that have reviewed the Stark Law produced written decisions of uncertain value, with some of the decisions giving less than fully accurate renditions of the law and the regulations.

The available guidance falls into three categories: (1) commentary in the Federal Register in connection with the various rulemakings; (2) CMS advisory opinions and frequently asked questions; and (3) case law. Each of these sources provides insight into how the Stark Law and the Stark Regulations are applied or viewed by CMS, other governmental agencies, and the courts. The various sources also present traps for the unwary due to, for example, changes in interpretation over time or incorrect statements in the available case law.

A. Regulatory Preambles and Commentary in the Federal Register

Why is the Federal Register important? It is the official journal of the federal government and is used by all government agencies for the publication of proposed and final rules as well as solicitations for comments from the public. Federal agencies are generally required to publish substantive rules in the Federal Register, and will often publish interpretive and procedural rules there as well. As such, the Federal Register is one of the only primary sources for government interpretations and pronouncements.

As explained in Chapter 2, there have been numerous rounds of regulations to get the Stark Regulations to their current form. Each round of regulations went through a proposal stage before being

---

1. Steven D. Wales, *The Stark Law: Boon or Boondoggle? An Analysis of the Prohibition on Physician Self-Referrals*, 27 L. & PSYCHOL. REV. 1, 22 (2003) (citations omitted).

encoded into a final rule. At both rule-making stages, proposed and final, CMS published introductory explanations and commentary in the Federal Register. The commentary from CMS sets out CMS's view of the regulations and how it may apply the regulations. This regulatory commentary is one of the most direct statements available from CMS on how to apply the Stark Law in practice. The comments are especially beneficial because they explain the sometimes vague language of the text of the regulations.

Just as the regulations evolved over time, so did the commentary. With certain exceptions, it is possible to see where CMS retreated on a restrictive approach or conversely took away a previously broad interpretation of the law. When analyzing a Stark issue, it is both necessary and informative to review the changes to a particular exception in order to understand how an arrangement or relationship may be structured to comply with the law.

The proposed rules contain an explanation from CMS for the purpose of a proposed change. The explanation provides a justification and basis for the change, which then invites comments and responses from interested parties. The final rules then contain "comments" and "responses," which essentially are a written dialogue between CMS and the parties that commented on a proposed rule, interim final rule, or final rule during a comment period. In the responses, CMS usually states whether it agrees or disagrees with a comment and then provides an explanation for its response. Examples of potential impacts may also be included with a CMS analysis of how it would respond to such a proposed relationship. Additionally, comments may influence how a rule is actually finalized. Accordingly, the comment and response dialogue in the Federal Register is often a very useful tool when performing a Stark analysis.

The rule-making publications with the majority of CMS commentary on Stark can be found as follows, which list includes proposed and final rules[2]:

- ◆ Stark II Proposed Rule—63 Fed. Reg. 1659 (Jan. 9, 1998)
- ◆ Stark II Phase I Final Rule—66 Fed. Reg. 856 (Jan. 4, 2001)

---

2. The rulemaking references in this Section focus upon the "Stark II" regulations.

- Stark II Phase II Interim Final Rule—69 Fed. Reg. 16,054 (Mar. 26, 2004)[3]
- CY 2008 Physician Fee Schedule—72 Fed. Reg. 38,122 (July 12, 2007)[4]
- Stark II Phase III Final Rule—72 Fed. Reg. 51,012 (Sept. 5, 2007)
- FY 2009 Inpatient Prospective Payment System Proposed Rule—73 Fed. Reg. 23,528 (Apr. 30, 2008)
- FY 2009 Inpatient Prospective Payment System Final Rule— 73 Fed. Reg. 48,434 (Aug. 19, 2008)
- CY 2011 Outpatient Prospective Payment System Proposed Rule—75 Fed. Reg. 46,431 (Aug. 3, 2010)
- CY 2011 Outpatient Prospective Payment System Final Rule—75 Fed. Reg. 71,799 (Nov. 24, 2010)
- CY 2012 Outpatient Prospective Payment System Proposed Rule—76 Fed. Reg. 42,349 (July 18, 2011)
- CY 2012 Outpatient Prospective Payment System Final Rule—76 Fed. Reg. 74,517 (Nov. 30, 2011)

The above list is not an all-encompassing list of the proposed and final rules impacting Stark. However, the above rules are the primary ones that have brought the Stark Regulations to their current form.

B. CMS Advisory Opinions

The Stark Law and the Stark Regulations require that CMS issue written advisory opinions upon request and submission by an interested party.[5] The Stark Regulations flesh out the process by which an advisory opinion may be requested, including the information that must be included in a request, the fees for obtaining an opinion,

---

3. No proposed rule was published for Phase II. Instead, CMS published Phase II as an "interim final rule," which became effective ninety days after its publication.
4. The CY 2008 Physician Fee Schedule contained some proposals that were finalized in the FY 2009 Inpatient Prospective Payment System Final Rule.
5. 42 U.S.C. § 1395nn(g)(6).

and a certification statement.[6] CMS has issued relatively few advisory opinions related to the Stark Law, but the few opinions available may still provide useful guidance in specific factual scenarios. Although an opinion is only binding on the requestor and as to the specific factual situations presented in the request,[7] the opinions nevertheless provide useful insights into how CMS will apply the legal standards of the Stark Law and which types of factual scenarios may be viewed as mundane or problematic.[8] Ultimately, it is important to remember that an advisory opinion cannot be legally relied upon by a third party, only the requestor.

C. Case Law

In addition to the Stark Law, the Stark Regulations, and advisory opinions, there is also limited case law interpreting the scope, application, and enforceability of all aspects of the Stark Law. Unfortunately, the case law is of limited utility because relatively few cases are filed and brought to a final decision. For those cases that proceed to an endpoint through actual litigation, the court often addresses only limited aspects of the Stark Law, misinterprets its complex requirements and related guidance, and does not offer binding precedent applicable beyond the very specific factual scenarios presented. The Supreme Court has not weighed in on a Stark question yet to create national precedent. Nonetheless, there appears to be an increasing amount of case law in recent years, and certain recent cases are worth noting.

1) *U.S. ex rel. Drakeford v. Tuomey Healthcare System*[9]
In May 2013, the jury in *Tuomey* returned a verdict finding that the defendant, Tuomey Health System (Tuomey), violated the Stark Law

---

6. 42 C.F.R. §§ 411.370–411.389.
7. 42 C.F.R. § 411.387.
8. Advisory opinions issued by CMS can be accessed at: http://www.cms.gov/Medicare/Fraud-and-Abuse/PhysicianSelfReferral/advisory_opinions.html.
9. United States *ex rel.* Drakeford v. Tuomey Healthcare Sys., Inc., 675 F.3d 394 (4th Cir. 2012) (the Fourth Circuit 2012 opinion actually contains a Stark analysis and commentary).

and the False Claims Act through certain indirect compensation arrangements with physicians, leading to $39 million in impermissible claims to Medicare.[10] At the time of publication, the final penalty for Tuomey's Stark violation had not yet been determined by the court, nor whether Tuomey would seek an appeal of the decision.

In *Tuomey,* Tuomey Healthcare System created a for-profit entity for the purposes of owning four limited liability companies that employed physicians part-time to provide certain outpatient surgeries and other procedures constituting designated health services. The physicians received salaries and performance incentives greater than the amounts the LLCs received for the procedures performed by those physicians. The physicians' employment agreements required that the physicians perform the covered procedures *exclusively* at Tuomey facilities, and stipulated that they were employees only during the time that they were performing the procedures. In addition to the payment for the procedures (the professional component), Tuomey also received payment for the technical fee (facility fee) associated with each procedure. The physicians received significant compensation from Tuomey that (through performance incentives) varied with the volume of referrals to Tuomey.

The government alleged that, in total through these LLC arrangements, Tuomey was losing between $1 and $2 million per year and that Tuomey would not have entered such arrangements without the additional revenue generated from the associated improper referrals to Tuomey.

Originally, the district judge imposed a $45 million penalty against Tuomey. The Fourth Circuit Court of Appeals overturned the judgment on procedural grounds (7th Amendment right to a jury trial). In reversing the district court, the Fourth Circuit addressed certain Stark Law issues in greater detail. Specifically, under the Stark Law, the Fourth Circuit held that: (1) a "referral" is generated in the context of inpatient and outpatient hospital services even when a physician personally performs the service because of the technical component of the service; and (2) contracts that value

---

10. United States *ex rel.* Drakeford v. Tuomey Healthcare Sys., Inc., Case No. 3:05-2858, jury verdict (D.S.C. May 8, 2013).

anticipated future referrals implicate the volume or value standard, which cannot be used when setting remuneration under Stark.

2) *U.S. ex rel. Singh v. Bradford Regional Medical Center*[11]

Bradford serves as an example both of the care entities must use in valuing arrangements implicating the Stark Law and of the difficulties courts have in analyzing Stark issues. Specifically, the arrangement that the court found violated the Stark Law was between a physician-owned medical practice and Bradford Regional Medical Center (Bradford). Under the suspect arrangement, Bradford subleased a nuclear camera from the medical practice, which was used to perform diagnostic tests constituting DHS,. Although this agreement did not require the physicians to refer patients to Bradford for the diagnostic testing, the evidence showed that the parties anticipated these referrals when considering the arrangement. For example, prior to the arrangement the physicians accounted for nearly half of such referrals to Bradford. Under the agreement, Bradford paid the medical practice a fixed "pass-through" amount for the lease, as well as a fixed fee for a non-compete portion of the agreement.

In analyzing the Stark Law implications of the arrangement, the court concluded that the lease was an indirect financial relationship between Bradford and the medical practice. Even though the fees were "fixed," the court concluded that the manner in which the fees were calculated considered variation with the volume and value of referrals because the fee was based on a calculation of expected revenues with the lease in place, less expected revenues without the lease in place. In an apparent conflation of the concept of volume or value of referrals with that of fair market value, the court found that this arrangement did not meet the definition of fair market value under the indirect compensation exception because the fee valued anticipated referrals.

---

11. United States *ex rel.* Singh v. Bradford Reg'l Med. Ctr., 752 F. Supp. 2d 602 (W.D. Pa., 2010).

3) *U.S. ex rel. Kosenske v. Carlisle HMA Inc. et al.*[12]

Kosenske presents another example of the importance of hearing evidence to support a fair market value determination under the Stark Law. *Kosenske* considered remuneration in the context of physician-hospital arrangements. The Third Circuit Court of Appeals held that an arrangement between an anesthesiology provider group and a hospital did not meet the requirements of the personal services exception, in part, because the parties did not satisfy the fair market value requirement and did not have a written arrangement for all items and services to be provided. Although the parties argued that their initial contract negotiations were adequate evidence that the agreement reflected fair market value, the Third Circuit rejected this argument, finding the fact that an arrangement is negotiated back and forth between the parties does not, per se, cause an arrangement to meet the Stark Law definition of fair market value. This case emphasized the importance of appropriately documenting (and updating documentation of) all aspects of arrangements implicating the Stark Law, including detailed evidence and support for the fair market value of the remuneration to be exchanged pursuant to an agreement.

4) *U.S. ex rel. Goodstein v. McLaren Regional Medical Center*[13]

Goodstein provides a good example of how courts may analyze fair market value for the purpose of Stark. In Goodstein, the parties agreed to limit the issue before the court to whether the lease amount in a physician office lease was set at fair market value. After hearing testimony from numerous experts on both sides, the court dismissed the complaint, finding that the lease was at fair market value. The most important evidence of an arm's-length transaction in the defense's favor was (1) the presence of a heated and lengthy negotiation of price and (2) McClaren's ability to secure various favorable terms in the lease. In addition, the primary flaws in the

---

12. United States *ex rel.* Kosenske v. Carlisle HMA Inc., 554 F.3d 88 (3d Cir. 2009).
13. United States *ex rel.* Goodstein v. McLaren Reg'l Med. Ctr., 202 F. Supp. 2d 671 (E.D. Mich. 2002).

government's evidence on fair market value were (1) the failure to consider relevant comparable buildings, (2) a too restrictive market area, and (3) not properly adjusting the analysis for the specific terms of McClaren's lease.

5) *U.S. ex rel. Villafane v. Solinger*[14]

Villafane is significant both because it is one of the few cases addressing the academic medical center exception to the Stark Law and because of its treatment of Medicaid under the Stark Law. First, the court took a pragmatic approach to the AMC exception in determining that various technical failures still satisfied the requirements of the exception. The court's approach differed from the usually rigid approach taken by many of the enforcement authorities when interpreting the Stark Law. The court found that the arrangement in question, involving an academic medical center and its faculty physicians, a free-standing hospital, and the medical school's foundation, could qualify for protection under the AMC exception even in light of various technical problems with the arrangement that may have warranted further scrutiny. In particular, the court was willing to overlook potential technical issues, including inaccurate timekeeping by faculty physicians, compensation to physicians at above the 75th percentile, and lack of detailed contracts documenting certain relationships between the relevant parties. Instead, the court focused on the overarching purpose of the Stark Law in preventing fraud and abuse.

Second, the *Villafane* court, without any additional analysis, implicitly brought Medicaid funds under the ambit of Stark Law liability. In its decision, the court noted that the parties acknowledged that the claims at issue involve only Medicaid (not Medicare) funds and stated that this fact did not impact the court's analysis of the case.[15] Such a statement directly contradicts the common understanding of Stark practitioners that Stark does not apply to Medicaid.

---

14. United States *ex rel.* Villafane v. Solinger, 543 F. Supp. 2d 678 (W.D. Ky. 2008).
15. *Id.* at n.3.

6) *U.S. ex rel. Baklid-Kunz v. Halifax Hospital Medical Center*

Halifax Hospital presents the importance of fully complying with all of the requirements of the bona fide employment exception. In particular, the compensation element and not taking the volume or value of referrals into account gave rise to the issue in *Halifax Hospital*. According to the relator, Halifax entered into employment agreements with several outside physicians that allegedly took the volume or value of referrals into account in setting the level of compensation paid to the physicians. The physicians received incentive compensation from a pool of funds that was divided among the physicians. In the complaint, the relator alleged that the physicians increased referrals in order to maximize the potential bonus because more patients meant a large potential pool.

To date, the *Halifax Hospital* case has produced two important decisions. The first was the Court's denial of Halifax's motion to dismiss, which focused on the connection between Stark and Medicaid.[16] In its motion to dismiss, Halifax argued that Stark could not serve as the basis for a claim under the False Claims Act concerning the allegedly improper Medicaid claims and reimbursements. In ruling against Halifax, the Court determined that the Medicaid statute prohibits States from receiving Federal Financial Participation (FFP) for Medicaid Services that were furnished pursuant to a referral that violate Stark if the service were a Medicare DHS. However, this decision means only that the Government's theory that Halifax caused the State to submit false claims is viable (assuming the claims were false). The Government would still need to prove that the hospital *knowingly* caused the State to submit false claims, which may be difficult to do, given that CMS signaled early on that the statutory prohibition against paying FFP was not self-implementing but rather needed regulations (which have not been issued). This Halifax decision has been followed by two other district courts.[17]

16. U.S. *ex rel* Baklid-Kunz v. Halifax Hospital Medical Center, 2012 WL 921147 (M.D. Fla. 2012).
17. *U.S. ex rel. Schubert v. All Children's Medical Center, Inc.*, 2013 U.S. Dist. LEXIS 163075 (M.D. Fla. Nov. 15, 2013); *U.S. ex rel. Parikh v. Citizens Medical Center*, 2013 U.S. Dist. LEXIS 134693 (S.D. Tex. Sept. 20, 2013).

The second important decision was issued in November 2013 when the Court ruled on a motion for partial summary judgment.[18] In its decision, the Court held that Halifax violated Stark by paying incentive bonuses that improperly took the volume or value of business into account. Halifax argued in vain that the incentive bonus was based upon services personally performed by the physicians, which is allowable under the bona fide employment exception, which permits productivity bonuses, that do not take into account, directly or indirectly, the volume or value of referrals. However, the Court accepted the government's argument that the bonus was *based* upon factors beyond just a physician's personally performed services, although the bonus was *divided* according to personally performed services. The Court specifically took issue with the fact that the bonus pool included DHS. Accordingly, the Court held that Halifax violated Stark.

---

18. U.S. *ex rel* Baklid-Kunz v. Halifax Hospital Medical Center, 2013 WL 6017329 (M.D. Fla. 2013).

Penalties and Compromise 4

Stark violations carry serious consequences ranging from monetary penalties to potential exclusion from participation in federal health care programs. Violations will also likely result in the denial of claims submitted and potential beneficiary refunds, depending upon the exact circumstances of a violation. While Stark itself contains only penalty provisions, a violation may also result in liability under other laws, including but not limited to the Civil Monetary Penalty (CMP) statute and False Claims Act (FCA). If a Stark problem is suspected, it is also possible to self-report the issue, which, like everything related to Stark, carries its own risks and rewards.

It is important to understand the scope of consequences associated with violating Stark. Knowing the implications of a violation can aid in advising individuals and entities in the health care field of the importance of adhering to Stark's requirements.

A. Sanctions

Payment for services billed to Medicare in violation of the Stark Law must be denied.[1] If claims submitted in violation of the law are paid in error, co-pays must be refunded to beneficiaries.[2] Where a knowing Stark violation has occurred, the HHS Office of the Inspector General (OIG) may seek to impose civil monetary penalties of up to $15,000 per improper claim and may exclude the offending physician and/or the DHS entity (depending on which party or parties had knowledge of the violation) from participation in federal health care programs.[3] Anyone who enters into an arrangement or scheme that he or she knows has a principal purpose of circumventing the Stark law is subject to civil monetary penalties of up to $100,000 per scheme and exclusion from federal health care programs.[4] An entity that furnishes Medicare services and, upon request from CMS or the OIG, fails to report relevant information regarding its financial relationships is subject to a penalty of $10,000 per day for each day the failure to report continues.[5] Such failure also may be grounds for exclusion from federal health care programs. A knowing violation of Stark is also a false claim for purposes of the FCA.

B. False Claims Act Liability

The FCA generally prohibits knowingly presenting or causing to be presented a false or fraudulent claim for payment by the federal government.[6] Knowing and intentional violations of Stark may lead to FCA liability. Parties that have allegedly intentionally set up arrangements to circumvent Stark or to directly not comply have been found liable under the FCA for submitting false or fraudulent claims that arose from those arrangements.

---

1. 42 U.S.C. § 1395nn(g)(1).
2. Id. at 1395nn(g)(2).
3. Id. at 1395nn(g)(3).
4. Id. at 1395nn(g)(4).
5. *Id.* at 1395nn(g)(5).
6. 31 U.S.C. §§ 3729-3733.

The Affordable Care Act created another means of imposing FCA liability for a Stark violation. Section 6402 of the Affordable Care Act requires a party to report and return an overpayment by the later of (1) sixty days of identifying the overpayment or (2) the date a corresponding cost report is due. An overpayment consists of any funds paid under a federal health care program to which the receiving entity or individual is not entitled. Given that a Stark violation results in the tainting of all payments, any payment received and retained pursuant to a non-compliant relationship or arrangement results in the receipt of overpayments.

On February 16, 2012, CMS published a proposed rule implementing the overpayment return requirement.[7] As under the Affordable Care Act, the proposed rule would require the return of overpayments within sixty days of identification. "Identify" was defined to mean having actual knowledge or acting with reckless disregard or deliberate ignorance of the existence of an overpayment. This definition introduced some clarity into an area of intense debate among Stark practitioners, but is itself controversial. The proposed rule also introduced the means by which an overpayment should be reported and returned. The proposed rule also suggested a ten-year look-back period for any overpayments, which exceeds the four-year reopening period for Medicare claims payments that were not fraudulently obtained,[8] and exceeds the usual six-year statute of limitations under the FCA[9] and CMP statute.[10] CMS has not yet published a final rule, but many comments were submitted, particularly on the length of the look-back period, and the proposal to define "identify" as including acting with reckless disregard or deliberate ignorance of the existence of an overpayment.

---

7. 77 Fed. Reg. 9179 (Feb. 16, 2012). No final rule has been released as of the date of publication.

8. 42 C.F.R. § 405.980(b).

9. 31 U.S.C. § 3731(b)(1). Paragraph (b)(2) provides that an action under the FCA may be brought up to ten years after the alleged false claim under certain, and rarely applicable, circumstances.

10. 42 U.S.C. § 1320a-7a(c)(1).

C. Self-Referral Disclosure Protocol

The Affordable Care Act created a Stark-specific Self-Referral Disclosure Protocol (SRDP) to allow parties to voluntarily report a Stark violation to CMS.[11] The SRDP was necessary for a number of reasons. For instance, the OIG, on May 29, 2009, stopped accepting into its self-disclosure protocol Stark violations that were unaccompanied by a colorable violation of the Anti-Kickback Statute,[12] which left parties without a clear avenue to self-report and resolve a Stark violation.

The purpose of the SRDP is to provide a procedure whereby Stark violations can be self-disclosed and the disclosing party can work with CMS to resolve the violation. As enacted in the Affordable Care Act, CMS has discretion to reduce the possible penalties associated with the disclosed Stark violation. The SRDP is for Stark violations only, not violations of any other law. If a party believes an arrangement may also involve a violation of the Anti-Kickback Statute or some other law, then the disclosure should occur elsewhere, such as the OIG or Department of Justice. Further, the SRDP is not part of CMS's advisory opinion process, which means that submissions should only be made for actual violations.

Entering the SRDP program stays a party's obligation to return suspected overpayments. Specifically, once a submission is accepted by CMS, the sixty-day period for returning overpayments created by Section 6402 of the Affordable Care Act is stayed. The stay continues so long as the party remains in the SRDP. This can be beneficial because CMS's ability to compromise the amount owed may enable a party to avoid returning the full amount resulting from a violation, depending upon the factors identified below.

CMS promulgated the initial SRDP on September 23, 2010, with technical corrections made on May 6, 2011. The SRDP sets forth the requirements for a submission into the program. Specifically, an SRDP submission must include, among other things: (1) the names and identifying information of the disclosing party, (2) a descrip-

---

11. Section 6409 of the Affordable Care Act required the Department of Health and Human Services to promulgate the SRDP.
12. It was also never certain whether the OIG had authority to resolve a suspected Stark violation.

tion of the nature of the matter being disclosed, (3) a statement explaining why the disclosing party believes a violation of Stark occurred, including a legal analysis of each element of every applicable Stark exception, (4) how the matter was discovered and what, if any, remedial measures have been taken, (5) a description of the existence and adequacy of any pre-existing compliance program, (6) whether the disclosed conduct is under current investigation or inquiry by another government agency or contractor, (7) a financial analysis relating to the matter being disclosed, and (8) a signed certification from the chief executive officer, chief financial officer, or other authorized representative.[13]

As stated above, CMS has the discretion to reduce penalties associated with self-disclosed conduct. When determining whether a reduction will occur, CMS may consider the following factors: "(1) the nature and extent of the illegal or improper practice; (2) the timeliness of the self-disclosure; (3) the cooperation in providing additional information related to the disclosure; (4) the litigation risk associated with the matter disclosed; and (5) the financial position of the disclosing party."[14]

CMS periodically posts settlements under the SRDP on its website. CMS does not provide much detail about each settlement beyond stating the amount of the settlement and a generalized description of the nature of the Stark violations reported.

---

13. The full Self-Referral Disclosure Protocol is available on CMS' website at: http://www.cms.gov/Medicare/Fraud-and-Abuse/PhysicianSelfReferral/Downloads/6409_SRDP_Protocol.pdf.
14. *Id.*

Resources and Reference Guide

Resources do exist that may assist in the interpretation and application of Stark. The resources identified below do not constitute a complete list, merely a few select resources.

A. ABA Health Law Section Resources

(1) The Stark & Anti-Kickback Toolkit—The toolkit is an electronic searchable database that includes narrative summaries, statutes, administrative history, regulations, administrative materials, links to the CMS website for Stark advisory opinions, links to the OIG website for anti-kickback advisory opinions, and several ABA Health Law Section publications.

(2) The Health Lawyer—A bimonthly scholarly publication analyzing a variety of issues in the health law field.

(3) Health eSource—A monthly electronic publication with shorter articles analyzing issues in the health law field.

(4) Health Care Fraud and Abuse: Practical Perspectives— A book containing an in-depth analysis of federal fraud and

abuse laws and regulations, including analyses of specific issues.

(5) Health Law Section Resources Page: www.americanbar.org/groups/health_law/resources.html

B. Government Resources

(1) Centers for Medicare and Medicaid Services: www.cms.gov
(2) CMS Physician Self-Referral Webpage: www.cms.gov/Medicare/Fraud-and-Abuse/PhysicianSelfReferral/index.html
(3) Office of the Inspector General of HHS: oig.hhs.gov

C. Federal Register Citations

(1) 1992 Proposed Rule—57 Fed. Reg. 8588 (Mar. 11, 1992)
(2) 1995 Final Rule—60 Fed. Reg. 41,914 (Aug. 14, 1995)
(3) Phase I Proposed Rule—63 Fed. Reg. 1659 (Jan. 9, 1998)
(4) Phase I Final Rule—66 Fed. Reg. 856 (Jan. 4, 2001)
(5) Phase II Interim Final Rule—69 Fed. Reg. 16,054 (Mar. 26, 2004)
(6) Phase II Correction Notice—69 Fed. Reg. 17,933 (Apr. 6, 2004)
(7) CY 2006 Physician Fee Schedule Proposed Rule—70 Fed. Reg. 45,764 (Aug. 8, 2005)
(8) Exceptions for Electronic Prescribing & Electronic Health Records Arrangements Proposed Rule—70 Fed. Reg. 59,182 (Oct. 11, 2005)
(9) CY 2006 Physician Fee Schedule Final Rule—70 Fed. Reg. 70,116 (Nov. 21, 2005)
(10) Exceptions for Electronic Prescribing & Electronic Health Records Arrangements Final Rule—71 Fed. Reg. 45,140 (Aug. 8, 2006)
(11) CY 2007 Physician Fee Schedule Proposed Rule—71 Fed. Reg. 48,982 (Aug.22, 2006)
(12) CY 2007 Physician Fee Schedule Final Rule—71 Fed. Reg. 69,688 (Dec. 1, 2006)

(13) CY 2008 Physician Fee Schedule Proposed Rule—72 Fed. Reg. 38,122 (July 12, 2007)

(14) FY 2008 Inpatient Prospective Payment System Final Rule—72 Fed. Reg. 48,169 (Aug. 22, 2007)

(15) Phase III Final Rule—72 Fed. Reg. 51,012 (Sept. 5, 2007)

(16) CY 2008 Physician Fee Schedule Final Rule—72 Fed. Reg. 66,222 (Nov. 27, 2007)

(17) FY 2009 Inpatient Prospective Payment System Proposed Rule—73 Fed. Reg. 23,528 (Apr. 30, 2008)

(18) CY 2009 Physician Fee Schedule Proposed Rule—73 Fed. Reg. 38,502 (July 7, 2008)

(19) FY 2009 Inpatient Prospective Payment System Final Rule—73 Fed. Reg. 48,434 (Aug. 19, 2008)

(20) CY 2009 Physician Fee Schedule Final Rule—73 Fed. Reg. 69,726 (Nov. 19, 2008)

(21) CY 2010 Physician Fee Schedule Proposed Rule—74 Fed. Reg. 33,520 (July 13, 2009)

(22) CY 2010 Physician Fee Schedule Final Rule—74 Fed. Reg. 61,738 (Nov. 25, 2009)

(23) CY 2010 Physician Fee Schedule Correction Notice & Final Rule—75 Fed. Reg. 26,356 (May 11, 2010)

(24) CY 2011 Physician Fee Schedule Proposed Rule—75 Fed. Reg. 40,140 (July 13, 2010)

(25) CY 2011 Outpatient Prospective Payment System Proposed Rule—75 Fed. Reg. 46,431 (Aug. 3, 2010)

(26) CY 2011 Outpatient Prospective Payment System Final Rule—75 Fed. Reg. 72,240 (Nov. 24, 2010)

(27) CY 2011 Physician Fee Schedule Final Rule—75 Fed. Reg. 73,443 (Nov. 29, 2010)

(28) CY 2012 Outpatient Prospective Payment System Proposed Rule—76 Fed. Reg. 42,349 (July 18, 2011)

(29) CY 2012 Outpatient Prospective Payment System Final Rule—76 Fed. Reg. 74,517 (Nov. 30, 2011)

D. Case Citations—For Court Opinions

(1) United States *ex rel.* Drakeford v. Tuomey Healthcare Sys., Inc., 675 F.3d 394 (4th Cir. 2012).

(2) United States *ex rel.* Singh v. Bradford Reg'l Med. Ctr., 752 F. Supp. 2d 602 (W.D. Pa., 2010).

(3) United States *ex rel.* Kosenske v. Carlisle HMA Inc. et al., 554 F.3d 88 (3rd Cir. 2009).

(4) United States *ex rel.* Goodstein v. McLaren Regional Medical Center, 202 F. Supp. 2d 671 (E.D. Mich. 2002).

(5) United States *ex rel.* Villafane v. Solinger, 543 F. Supp. 2d 678 (W.D. Ky. 2008).